PETERSON'S

Game
Plan for
Getting
into

Medical

School

C. S. Jewell

Peterson's
Thomson Learning™

Australia • Canada • Denmark • Japan • Mexico
New Zealand • Philippines • Puerto Rico • Singapore
Spain • United Kingdom • United States

About Peterson's

Founded in 1966, Peterson's, a division of Thomson Learning, is the nation's largest and most respected provider of lifelong learning online resources, software, reference guides, and books. The Education Supersite^{SM} at petersons.com—the Web's most heavily traveled education resource—has searchable databases and interactive tools for contacting U.S.-accredited institutions and programs. CollegeQuest^{SM} (CollegeQuest.com) offers a complete solution for every step of the college decision-making process. GradAdvantage^{TM} (GradAdvantage.org), developed with Educational Testing Service, is the only electronic admissions service capable of sending official graduate test score reports with a candidate's online application. Peterson's serves over 55 million education consumers annually.

Thomson Learning is among the world's largest providers of lifelong learning information. Headquartered in Stamford, CT, with multiple offices worldwide, Thomson Learning is a division of The Thomson Corporation (TTC), one of the world's leading information companies. TTC operates mainly in the U.S., Canada, and the UK and has annual revenues of over US$6 billion. The Corporation's common shares are traded on the Toronto, Montreal, and London stock exchanges. For more information, visit TTC's Internet address at www.thomcorp.com.

Visit Peterson's Education Center on the Internet (World Wide Web) at www.petersons.com

Library of Congress Cataloging-in-Publication Data

Jewell, Cathy S., 1967 -
    Game plan for getting into medical school / by Cathy S. Jewell.
       p. cm.
    ISBN 0-7689-0393-9
    1. Medical colleges—United States—Admission. 2. Medical colleges—United States—
       Entrace requirements. 3. Medicine—Vocational guidance—United States. I. Title

  R838.4 .J49 2000
  610'.71'173—dc21   99-087860

Printed in Canada

10 9 8 7 6 5 4 3 2 1

Contents

INTRODUCTION   **1**

CHAPTER 1: GETTING STARTED   **7**
Setting Personal Goals   7
Why Medicine?   8
General Information on Medical Schools   9
Time Line   21

CHAPTER 2: POSITIONING YOURSELF AS A PROSPECTIVE MEDICAL STUDENT   **25**
Planning in High School   25
Planning in College   28
Admission Requirements   31

CHAPTER 3: SELECTING A MEDICAL SCHOOL   **49**
Where to Start   49
Identifying Schools and Criteria   50
Early Decision Programs   62
Combined Programs   63
Visiting Schools   64
Making a Short List   65
The Application   67

CHAPTER 4: THE APPLICATION PROCESS   **69**
What Do Medical Schools Want?   69
Types of Applications   69
Elements of an Application   74
How to Keep It All Organized   88
How to Decide which School to Attend   89
What to Do if You Don't Get In (This Time)   91

CHAPTER 5: PAYING FOR MEDICAL SCHOOL   **95**
Costs Associated with Medical School   95
Paying For It: Introduction to Financial Aid   105
Sources of Financial Aid   111

Where To Go?   127
A Final Word on Budgets   128

CHAPTER 6: ONCE YOU'RE THERE   **131**
Adjusting   131
Courses (and the Tried-and-True Methods of Getting
  through Them)   132
Clinical Study   133
Stress (and Release)   135
Words of Advice   136

**APPENDIX A: MEDICAL SCHOOLS AND
THEIR AFFILIATED HOSPITALS**   **139**

**APPENDIX B: AMCAS AND AACOMAS
SAMPLE APPLICATIONS**   **175**

APPENDIX C: SAMPLE APPLICATION ESSAYS   **185**

APPENDIX D: USEFUL WEB SITES   **193**

**APPENDIX E: PRINT RESOURCES USED IN
THIS VOLUME**   **195**

T he institution of the medical school in the United States has evolved to its current position over the last two centuries. From medieval times through the eighteenth century, most doctors learned their trade through an apprenticeship. In Europe, students would apprentice to a master for five to seven years, after which they were admitted to a guild with a license to practice medicine. Only the elite had access to university training, after which they would hold an academic degree and could become teachers or work in government. Some European countries required physicians to acquire academic qualifications in order to practice medicine, and through government bureaucracy, physicians essentially obtained a territory, or town, in which they held the exclusive right to practice medicine. In eighteenth-century England, however, regulation was quite lax outside of London, and medical education was not widely available. No medical licensing system was in place, and market forces were relied upon to regulate the medical practice—if one seemed to offer good services for inexpensive prices, one's business might succeed. The market could be fickle, however, and without regulation, physicians had no job security and no recourse against charlatans purporting to hold magical medical cures for ailments.

Perhaps naturally, the medical system that evolved in the U.S. was similar to that in England at the time. There were no university requirements and no guilds. The elite in the U.S. went to Europe to receive university medical training. The first major development influencing U.S. medical training was the publication in 1765 of *Discourse upon the Institution of Medical Schools in America*, by John Morgan. A Philadelphian, Morgan received his physician's training in Edinburgh, Scotland. An education at Edinburgh University, which was well respected for the modern medical education it provided, offered clinical training in an infirmary (a practice pioneered there), as well as the basic elements necessary for the practice of medicine and surgery: anatomy, chemistry, medical theory, and surgery. Morgan wrote concerning the importance of qualifying examinations for physicians, which would ensure that all practicing physicians met minimum standards of instruction. Also in 1765, Monroe established the department of medicine at the University of Pennsylvania and assumed the department chair of what would become the first U.S. medical school.

Though some groups of doctors tried to establish minimum standards, the U.S. government was not supportive of restrictive regulation, and regulation evolved slowly, state by state. Twenty years after Harvard's medical school was established in 1783, Massachusetts began requiring either a Harvard diploma or a qualifying exam for a Massachusetts license. Connecticut instituted similar regulations in 1810, as did South Carolina in 1817. There was still no nationwide regulation of physicians, however, and U.S. expansion westward led to physician shortages, which in turn led untrained settlers to practice medicine, often relying on mail-order home medical kits.

In 1874, Dr. Andrew Taylor Still founded the first osteopathic medical school in Kirksville, Missouri. Osteopathy taught a philosophy of whole body natural health; Dr. Still believed that all parts and functions of the body were interrelated and that the body was naturally healthy and could often repair itself. By 1876, there were sixty-two commercial medical schools in the U.S.; these institutions were intended to produce doctors quickly for a fee. There were also eleven homeopathic medical schools and four classified simply as "eclectic" (Porter 1998). The American Medical Association (founded in 1847) served as a base for academic physicians, who could do little to slow down the production of poorly trained doctors by the private, unregulated medical schools until early in the twentieth century, when scientific medicine became more popular in the U.S. In 1896 at Columbia University, X-rays were first taken for medical diagnosis. Medical research projects were privately financed by such wealthy benefactors as John D. Rockefeller and Andrew Carnegie.

In 1910, Abraham Flexner published his critique of the U.S. medical education system, *Medical Education in the United States and Canada*. Flexner, who was educated at Johns Hopkins and the University of Berlin, advocated reducing the number of medical schools in the U.S. and raising the standards of those that remained. He believed the best medical schools were in urban areas, which had better clinical training resources, and that they should be attached to universities, encouraging the production of research and providing students with solid science backgrounds that would be better provided at universities with the proper resources and facilities for such training. Flexner felt that entry requirements to medical schools should be stringent and that the education should culminate with a doctoral degree.

Within ten years of publication of Flexner's volume, forty-six medical schools closed, including most of the schools for black and women students (Porter 1998). The departments that remained for the most part followed Flexner's advice, affiliating with universities and hospitals and engaging in scientific training and research. Foundations such as the Rockefeller Institute for Medical Research began supporting university-based medical programs and projects, and such funding helped the new system to prosper. Medical faculty members became full-time teachers rather than practicing physicians, and clinical research performed at affiliated university hospitals became a part of the academic medical institution. In 1930, the former federal bacteriological laboratory at the Staten Island Marine Hospital moved to Bethesda, Maryland, and was renamed the National Institutes of Health (Porter 1998). The NIH became a research center, moving medical research firmly into the public sphere.

Fewer medical institutions meant fewer doctors, of course, and this resulted in a demand for physicians, whose status and salaries increased. The American Medical Association (AMA) also gained status and power and recommended medical cures for a variety of ills. The U.S. economy was good, and people were visiting doctors for basic and emergency care, as well as for elective surgeries (according to Porter, the 1920s have been called "the golden age for tonsillectomies"). Health insurance became an issue, and federally funded health programs were begun under Franklin Roosevelt's post-Depression New Deal era. The AMA resisted such programs, which could contain costs and take income and control out of the hands of individual physicians.

In 1929, the first fixed-rate group medical plan was provided for school teachers in Dallas by Baylor University Hospital; Blue Cross and Blue Shield followed in the early 1930s with prepaid hospital benefit programs. From 1940 to 1960, private health insurance became a large and profitable business in the U.S.; a growing middle class purchased health plans, or their employers did so (Porter 1998). Private insurance companies gained the position of great power in American medicine that they continue to hold.

Medical schools today are all well regulated and accredited, and they continue to follow the model espoused by Abraham Flexner in 1910. Of course, the nature of medicine has continued to change: technology has been responsible for many medical advancements and countless treatments, and the insurance industry has also been transformed to include the managed-care industry, which now increasingly dominates the U.S. medical system. Most medical schools now incorporate facets of managed care into their curricula (Comarow 1999). Medical schools have seen increased numbers of applicants in the past decade, though the number of accepted applicants has been slowly decreasing. The number of new applicants peaked in 1996–97 and has been slowly declining since; in 1998–99, there were 41,004 applicants to allopathic medical schools (MSAR 1999). Yet despite an overall physician surplus, there remain physician shortages in urban and rural areas of the U.S., which the U.S. Department of Health and Human Services has labeled Health Professional Shortage Areas (HPSA).

The U.S. medical school system and the health-care system in general have changed dramatically in recent decades, but for those committed to the practice of medicine and the service of others, the medical professions remain a valid and rewarding option. This volume is a resource for those who are interested in the medical field, considering a medical career, or planning to apply to medical school.

Getting Started

Chapter 1

SETTING PERSONAL GOALS

Why become a doctor? Do you want to be a doctor because your mother or father is one? Because of the high-income and high-prestige potential? Because it is the most difficult course of study you can follow? Or do you truly love biology, anatomy, and chemistry? Do you want to help people and serve a community? Before taking the Medical College Admission Test (MCAT) and applying to medical schools, be sure that this is the path you want to take and not one you will follow because your parents or guidance counselor want this career for you. You can do many things with your degree in biology (or Italian literature), but it will be more difficult for you to change your mind farther down the road when you have an M.D. or are two years toward one (with tens of thousands of dollars in student loan debt to accompany your education). Medical school is a long, arduous, and costly path to follow, and you should be certain of your commitment to medicine before taking all those science prerequisites, working hard on the MCAT, and applying to extremely competitive medical programs.

> "You learn a trade in medical school; the art is something you usually develop on your own or through chance encounters with a unique mentor."
>
> —former medical student, University of California, San Diego, School of Medicine

Your struggle to practice medicine will not necessarily end once you have graduated from medical school. U.S. Department of Health and Human Services figures indicate that the United States currently has a 29 percent surplus of physicians. The surplus is even greater in some areas of specialization and is at least 40 percent in the fields of gastroenterology, medical ontology, and hematology (Brink 1999). If you decide that you still want to go into medicine, research your area of specialization carefully to ensure that you will find a job when you finish your residency. Medicine remains a prestigious field, and it is relatively high paying, though you should definitely not go into medicine for the money. The median income for physicians is over $160,000 per year. This is the median; physicians in some specialties and those who work in particular regions of the United States command considerably more or less than the average. Keep in mind that before you are able to make a physician's salary, you must make it through your residency of three to eight years for which, as a first-year resident, you can expect an annual salary of approximately $30,000 to $35,000.

> "Look at the future of medicine before going to medical school. Several of my classmates have left medicine for [careers in] business . . . a waste of time and money."
>
> —medical student, Yale University School of Medicine

WHY MEDICINE?

Why you want to pursue a medical career is a very important question for you to consider, and it is one that will inevitably be asked of you again and again by your premedical counselor, in your application essay, and in your medical school interviews. Consider why you want to become a doctor and be able to express your answer clearly and succinctly. Not only the fact that you want to be a doctor but also why you want to become a doctor tells others a great deal about you. Were you drawn to medicine after a relative faced an illness or accident? By a wonderful family physician? Have you always tried to help others? If you cannot answer this question, stop reading now and find your answer. Perhaps you don't really want to be a doctor after all. If you truly do, you should know why. If you haven't considered this question thoroughly and are asked to answer it in an interview, your mechanical or unthoughtful answer will reflect very poorly on you and will not encourage any school to accept you, even if your grade point average (GPA) and MCAT scores are high. Medical schools are accepting the total package that is you, not simply the numbers that you have to represent yourself.

GENERAL INFORMATION ON MEDICAL SCHOOLS

The medical school admission process is extremely competitive. A few decades ago, you could be certain, if you were a good student and had done relatively well on the MCAT, that you would be accepted to a few medical schools. This is no longer the case. Today, you must start planning for admission very early and work hard to make yourself a standout candidate in order to procure a coveted slot at one of the 125 U.S. medical schools. For 1998–99 admission, 41,004 students applied for 16,170 positions in medical school. Do the math: about 39 percent of applicants were accepted to medical school—first-time applicants had a 45.9 percent acceptance rate. (Actually, 42.4 percent of all candidates were accepted; 39 percent of all accepted applicants enrolled. Medical schools commonly make more offers of admission than there are spaces, with the expectation that some students will decline the offer of admission.) Students may be heartened to know that in 1998–99, there was a 9.5 percent decrease in the number of applicants since 1994–95, when only 36 percent of applicants were accepted (MSAR 1999). More than 39 to 42 percent of applicants may be well qualified, but with so few positions, many good students will be rejected. With this kind of competition, you must make yourself an outstanding applicant in all regards if you want to get into medical school.

> "College is fun. Med school is work."
>
> —medical student, Yale University School of Medicine

Admission

When choosing the schools to which you will apply, you should be realistic. If your grades were only pretty good and your MCAT scores were OK, you should probably not apply to the most competitive medical school programs. Check out the various rankings, but do not invest too much in them. They may serve as a general guideline for you, but the criteria used to rank schools vary and will not likely give the same weight that you might to categories of consideration, such as acceptance rates, the faculty-student ratio, and the amount of research funding received.

According to the *Medical School Admission Requirements* (MSAR), an annual guide published by the Association of American Medical Colleges (AAMC), for the class entering in 1998–99, Boston University had more than 10,000 applicants for 143 positions. Harvard, however, had only 3,463 applicants for 165 positions. Does this mean you are more likely to get into Harvard? Probably not. You must look carefully at schools before deciding where to apply. Harvard indicates under the selection factors section in the MSAR that its accepted applicants in 1998 had an average GPA of 3.8, and MCAT scores averaged 10.8 on verbal reasoning, 12 on physical sciences, and 11.9 on biological sciences. If you are not an excellent candidate for medical school, Harvard may not be your best bet. Choose schools whose competitive criteria you meet. If you worked on a project to find a vaccine for AIDS or you started a clinic in a Third-World, war-torn country, your chances of acceptance at Johns Hopkins University will be good, even if your MCAT scores were so-so. However, if you do not have such amazing activities on your resume, your MCAT scores are straight 8s, and your GPA is a 3.0, you should probably not apply to a school with criteria similar to Harvard or Johns Hopkins.

On the other hand, don't sell yourself short. Please do not hesitate to apply to schools with programs that fit your demonstrated interests, even if your GPA was not what it should have been in those first two years of college. If you are one of those students whose freshman and sophomore grades hurt your GPA but whose grades improved vastly in your junior and senior years, your MCAT scores are good, and your activities show your interest in medicine and your fit with their program, then by all means apply to programs whose average scores for acceptance are a little higher than yours. Be sure to explain in your essay why you are a great candidate for their program, those early grades notwithstanding. Most admission committees are looking for good students who are well rounded and have a demonstrated interest in medicine. If you worked your way through school and your GPA suffered slightly, your maturity and demonstrated responsibility, along with your MCAT scores and other elements of your application, may go a long way toward compensating for your less-than-stellar grades.

Technology

Today, technology and medicine go hand in hand. Are you the kind of student who wants to be on top of the latest medical technology and computer innovations? Whether you answer yes or no, this is a factor you should consider when researching medical schools. Check into the curricula of the medical schools you are considering to find out if computer-assisted learning is utilized. See which hospitals the school has an affiliation with, which may help you determine the kind of clinical experience you will receive.

Medical Advances

As you may be aware, medical technology is rapidly advancing, and new fields are being created because of the influence of technology. In recent decades, ultrasound has become a widely used diagnostic tool, human organ transplants have become nearly commonplace, and researchers have also attempted to genetically engineer pigs to produce organs for transplant to human beings. Genetic research has also resulted in the mapping of genes, the cloning of sheep, the discovery of genes that cause genetic illnesses, and the production of genetically engineered human insulin. New drug therapies are available to treat everything from cancer to heart disease to AIDS. Surgeons are no longer operating with rudimentary implements such as the scalpel but are using lasers and endoscopes with fiber optics to perform less-invasive surgical procedures. Magnetic resonance imaging (MRI) is also allowing surgeons to perform minimally invasive and noninvasive medical procedures. Procedures that were brand new only a few decades ago are now commonplace across the U.S., including laser surgery to correct nearsightedness and in vitro fertilization as an infertility treatment.

New Fields, New Skills

What does all of this mean to you as a prospective medical student? It means that there are many more fields of specialty from which you may choose, and also that the training you receive as a medical student will be much more technical than it was twenty or thirty years ago. If you want to be a surgeon today, you should be prepared to train on endoscopic equipment and to update your skills as technology continues its rapid advance. For some students, this is very exciting news, and others see it as the end of medicine as we know it. However you feel, you must accept that technology will be an important part of the resources you have at your disposal as a medical doctor. While you may not have to use ultrasound equipment in your specialty, you will have to keep up with the latest innovations as it becomes a more common diagnostic tool.

If you are not interested in the more high-technology advances in medicine, you may want to look for a school where this is not the focus, but know that you will not likely have an easy time in medical school if you are computerphobic. Patient simulators are often used to help students learn diagnostic skills before they begin their clinical experience, and computers (and the Internet) are a necessary part of most library research and paper writing you will do. Computers are changing medicine in many ways, as evidenced by the field of medical informatics, which is essentially medical computer science. This field is changing the systems of medical record keeping. Just as the card catalog has disappeared from most university libraries, paper medical records may soon be almost completely replaced by electronic records. You will need to understand such systems of record keeping in order to access your patients' medical records and perhaps provide life-saving information to doctors in other states (or countries). The Mayo medical system has already created paperless systems for medical record keeping in Jacksonville and Arizona (Yacoe 1999). There are Internet drugstores, and many Internet information resources for diagnosing illness as well as researching papers. If you are interested in technology, try to pinpoint those programs that offer courses utilizing computers and other technology in their medical training or are affiliated with hospitals or research centers that are technologically advanced.

Hospitals and Other Facilities

When comparing medical schools, it is important to consider the medical facilities associated with the university. Does the program have a teaching hospital or an affiliation with one? You can look into rankings when researching medical schools, but again, these will not necessarily be of great use to you, because rankings tell you nothing about the specific facilities the top-ranked schools have. *U.S. News & World Report* publishes an issue on the best hospitals in the U.S., but this is geared toward patients rather than medical students. This publication can be helpful to you in determining the medical specialties of various hospitals. The type of hospital associated with your medical school is very important, because much of your clinical training will likely take place there. Is it an urban hospital? A

Veterans Administration (VA) hospital? A well-known research institution? An urban hospital may have a greater focus on emergency medicine than a rural hospital, a VA hospital is a place where you will receive a great deal of hands-on learning, and a research facility may be well equipped and have big-name physicians on its staff. You will find your clinical experience shaped by the hospital or other facility in which you receive your clinical education, and this may lead you toward or away from certain specialties. In addition, the clerkships you take will provide you with the experience to make you a better residency candidate; if you want a residency in geriatric medicine, be sure to attend a medical school with the clinical facilities to provide you with a geriatric clerkship, and check with the school so that you know such a clerkship is possible (more information on clerkships is available later in this chapter). The MSAR provides information (as provided by the institutions) on the teaching facilities each medical school is associated with, and a listing of these facilities can also be found in Appendix A. This information is subject to change, so be sure to check with the medical schools as well.

Degrees

The prevalent system of medical training in the United States is the M.D., or Doctor of Medicine; this volume focuses on the M.D. admission process. However, the D.O., or Doctor of Osteopathy degree, should also be considered an option for those applying to medical school. While most U.S. medical schools (125 schools, including three in Puerto Rico) teach allopathic medicine (toward the M.D.), osteopathic medicine is taught at nineteen schools in the U.S. (leading to the D.O. degree). These two types of degrees are taught by different schools: you cannot get an M.D. from an osteopathy school, nor can you get a D.O. at an allopathic school. The differences between these programs are many, but in the end, with either an M.D. or a D.O., you are a trained doctor and can treat patients, prescribe medications, and work in a hospital or in private practice alongside other M.D.'s and D.O.'s.

Osteopathy

Originally, osteopathic medicine was based on the musculoskeletal system and its effect on the rest of the body. Students were trained to manipulate the skeletal system in order to alter the course of disease, cure disease, or treat pain. This training program remains the more holistic approach to medicine, and students today are taught to consider the ways in which the different bodily systems are interrelated and affect one another. Dr. Andrew Taylor Still developed the osteopathic "whole body" approach in 1874 and founded the first osteopathic school of medicine in 1892 in Kirksville, Missouri. Perhaps because of this whole body approach, osteopathic doctors tend toward general practice, family practice, and internal medicine. If you study osteopathic medicine, you may specialize in another area and are eligible for internships and residencies at non-osteopathic hospitals. Opinions vary on whether you are at a competitive disadvantage in applying for such residencies when you graduate from an osteopathic school. The osteopathic course of study is a four-year program, with courses and curricula quite similar to M.D. programs, but highly selective residencies may be likely to choose M.D.'s before D.O.'s, making it unlikely that a student with an osteopathic degree will receive one of the highly competitive surgical residencies.

There are a few points in favor of osteopathy. On average, osteopathic programs accept students with slightly lower MCAT scores and GPAs than allopathic programs. Osteopathic schools are more likely to accept nontraditional students and to credit community college course work. If you are considering osteopathic medicine, you should research specific schools and, before applying, be certain that this type of medicine is what you really want to study. You are not likely to get into an osteopathic school if you obviously know nothing about this course of study and are applying only as a backup plan. Note that there are many fewer osteopathic than allopathic schools, and the application process is different than that for allopathic schools. See Chapter 4 for more on the application process, and contact the American Association of Colleges of Osteopathic Medicine (AACOM) for application guidelines and a complete list of osteopathic medical schools (AACOM, 5550 Friendship Boulevard, Suite 310, Chevy Chase, Maryland 20815-7231; telephone: 301-968-4100; Web site: http://www.aacom.org).

Types of Medical Training

Curriculum and teaching methods are important considerations when selecting a medical school. The program you choose will provide you with the foundations for your medical career and will give you the experience you need to prepare you for your U.S. Medical Licensing Examinations (USMLE) as well as your residency. You should be certain that the curriculum will meet your needs and that the methods and teaching philosophy of the school will work for you. Most programs use the lecture or seminar and laboratory methods in the first two years of training, followed by the clerkship in years three and four, but these are by no means the only kinds of training. The common training methods used by medical schools are described in detail below.

Years One and Two: Preclinical Training

Lectures and Seminars

These are the most common core methods of teaching and follow the model you will recall from your undergraduate training. Lectures and seminars provide the student with the majority of his or her preclinical training in the basic sciences. This method varies from program to program, but not a great deal. There are questions you should consider regarding lectures and seminars. Are more courses offered in a lecture format or in smaller seminars? Are the courses required by your program offered in one format exclusively? How well do you perform in smaller group discussions? Are you a good team player, or do you prefer to work on your own? Small groups require teamwork and encourage student participation, but, as a labor-intensive method for faculty members, these are less commonly offered during the first year or two of medical training. Work in small groups is more common during a student's clinical studies. Most medical schools using the lecture format will have one session of the required courses for all students—you may find yourself in a class of 100 or more students (your entire entering class)—for introductory courses. Below are some of the additional methods used in your lecture and seminar courses.

Preclinical Training Tools

Laboratory experience   Part of your preclinical training, and a supplement to some of your lecture courses, is your laboratory work. Generally a requirement, laboratory experience in medical school will seem familiar to most medical students, who likely have undergraduate experience in the sciences. The laboratory is a large part of the student's preclinical training and may include a lecture component as well as small-group discussions.

Case studies   The use of sample patient cases is a helpful tool in assessing and treating disease. With actual or fictional case histories, students evaluate symptoms and diagnose "patients," determining a proposed course of treatment. Less hands-on than working with patients (or simulated patients), this method nonetheless provides practical experience with clinical evaluation for medical students.

Problem-based learning   This is a recent addition to medical teaching methods. Small groups of students work together on case studies under the supervision of a faculty member. Individual students report to the group on specific aspects of the case; the team works together to understand clinical procedures and disease pathologies, honing the skills required for clinical practice.

Computer-based instruction   Most students will have a level of computer literacy upon entering medical school, and computers are more and more a tool with which faculty members and students feel comfortable. Many schools are utilizing computers to provide students with diagnostic exercises and case studies as well as CD-ROM course work. Students are generally expected to be familiar with word processing programs and to be able to work with reference databases for course research. A number of programs require that students purchase a specific type of computer upon entering the program; the student will be informed of this requirement prior to entering the program.

Years Three and Four: Clinical Training

Clinical Assessment and Direct Patient Experience

Supervised hands-on experience with patients is something many students long for and others dread. Clinical training is not normally offered until after the first two years of training, when students are well versed in the basics of medicine and are prepared to diagnose disease in human patients. Some programs, however, introduce students to clinical training as early as the first year of study. (The use of computer-simulated patients or human actors may be a complement to experience with actual patients.) The clinical course of study can be extremely useful to students in determining their specialization; it will afford you the opportunity to fine-tune your bedside manner and may lead you to an area of specialization that particularly interests you.

Clinical Training Tools

Clerkships   The clerkship, which will serve as an integral part of the medical student's clinical training, is routinely introduced in the third year of study and lasts from six to twelve weeks. The student will clerk in a hospital or private practice, working either as a member of a ward team or one-on-one with a physician. Clinical experience is supervised by a physician at the clinical facility, who is usually called a preceptor. During clerkships the student will have the opportunity to work directly with patients, gaining hands-on experience and exercising the clinical and diagnostic skills he or she learned in the first two years of study. Clerkships usually take place in the hospitals and research facilities with which the medical school is affiliated, so prospective medical students should be certain that the school they choose to attend is affiliated with at least two such teaching facilities and that the facilities will be appropriate to the specialization the student wishes to study.

Core clerkships   Students are required to complete clerkships in a number of core areas of specialization (including medicine, obstetrics and gynecology, pediatrics, psychiatry, and surgery) as part of their training program, and a certain number of elective clerkships are also usually required. If you are interested in a particular area of specialty, be sure that the medical schools you apply to offer clerkships (either required or elective) in those areas so that you will be able to gain clinical experience in your areas of interest. Required and elective clerkships vary from school to school and should give you a wide variety of clinical experience. You may find out, when completing your pediatric clerkship, that this is the area in which you would like to specialize. In addition to the core clerkships mentioned above, possible required and elective clerkships include ambulatory medicine, anesthesiology, cardiology, critical care, dermatology, emergency medicine, ethics, family medicine, gastroenterology, genetics, geriatrics, hematology, infectious diseases, nephrology, neurology, nutrition, ophthalmology, orthopedics, otolaryngology, pathology, plastic surgery, primary care, public health, radiology, rehabilitation medicine, substance abuse, and urology.

Independent study   If you are a self-motivated student with a clear idea of your interests and goals, a program that includes independent study courses may be just what you want. Students work in conjunction with a faculty member to design the independent course of study that involves a research project, with readings approved by the faculty adviser, and may include clinical experience. Because of the nature of this method, it is usually offered only after the first two years of study have been completed and is not often a required aspect of training. The independent study may be used to supplement clerkship experience or to gain experience not offered in the medical school's core and elective clerkships.

Internships   Some programs offer elective internships to provide students with on-site experience with a physician in their chosen area of specialization. Internships are useful in providing the student with an idea of the daily work life of a physician in an office or hospital setting and are practical for more self-directed learners. Internships generally supplement a student's clerkship experiences, but, as with independent study work, they can also be used to cover an area of specialization in which a clerkship is unavailable.

Preceptorships   This term is used variably; as mentioned above, your clinical supervisor is often called a preceptor, and some schools may call a clerkship a preceptorship. A medical student may have a preceptor who acts as an adviser and mentor to the student during the student's years of medical school study. The preceptorship may also be more like the traditional apprenticeship/mentorship program. This is a course of study whereby the student selects a preceptor in a given field and apprentices with that person for a set period of time. Preceptorships may be clinical or research in nature and provide the student with valuable one-on-one experience. Your chosen school may use preceptors in any of these capacities.

Other Teaching Methods

Multimedia presentations, contextual learning, and a variety of other methods may complete the training program offered at your school of choice. Methods other than those discussed above are not typically a major component of the program of study, and prospective students should contact medical schools directly for a complete listing and description of teaching methods implemented.

It is important to select a program that fits your style of learning; small-group discussion and independent study may be perfect if you are a self-starter, but if you require a more structured learning environment, the more traditional lecture–case study program may be best for you. Also remember that programs may be more or less centered on hands-on experience with patients; some programs are less immersing and stick to lectures and labs for at least the first two years of medical training. Do you learn well in group situations? What kinds of clerkships would you like to have? Check each program to see what it has to offer and apply to those that best suit your needs.

Special Programs

In addition to a variety of teaching methods, many schools offer special programs or research opportunities that may be of interest to you. This information, as well as complete information on teaching methods and curriculum, is available from the medical school program. Request catalogs and search the Web sites of the departments in which you are interested. The MSAR includes detailed program descriptions, and the AAMC also publishes an annual Curriculum Directory that lists year-by-year course and clerkship requirements for each U.S. and Canadian medical school. You should rely on the medical school materials directly, however, to be certain of what each program has to offer. Finally, be clear on why you have chosen each program: you may be asked about this in your interview. In the next chapter, we will begin planning for medical school admission.

TIME LINE

High School/Early College

- Get the MSAR.
- Review admission requirements.
- Research medical schools.

Freshman Year in College

- Meet with your premedical adviser at least twice.
- Enroll in a yearlong science course to fulfill admission requirements.

- Explore extracurricular activities (perhaps including volunteer work at a hospital or nursing home).

Summer

- Continue your medical school research.
- Travel.
- Work with a family doctor.

Sophomore Year in College

- Enroll in another one to two required sciences courses.
- Meet with your premed adviser at least twice.
- Join or organize a premed student union
- Continue activities.

Summer

- Get a research internship.
- Work in a local hospital.

Junior Year in College

- Meet with your premed adviser at least twice.
- Enroll in one to two required courses (plan to be finished with the prerequisites by the end of your junior year).
- Start looking into scholarships for medical school.
- Begin studying for the MCAT.
- In January, get information and register for the MCAT.
- In April, take the MCAT.

Summer

- During May and June, finalize, with your adviser's assistance, your list of approximately twelve schools to which you will apply; request three to five letters of recommendation from professors, your adviser, faculty members of medical schools, and/or doctors with whom you have worked; and work on your application essay.

- In June, receive your MCAT scores, complete your essay, and work on your American Medical College Application Service (AMCAS) application and other applications.
- In July, turn in your AMCAS application.
- In August, retake the MCAT, if necessary.

Senior Year in College

- Start receiving interview requests and secondary application materials from interested medical schools.
- Have a practice interview with your premed adviser.
- Work on secondary applications.
- Get all of your recommendation letters.
- Go on interviews.
- Turn in all secondary materials and check with schools to be certain your application files are complete.
- Continue all activities.
- In January and February, check financial aid information and due dates for possible schools and complete and turn in your Free Application for Federal Student Aid (FAFSA).
- In May, choose your school, graduate from college, and get ready to enter medical school.

Positioning Yourself as a Prospective Medical Student

Chapter 2

PLANNING IN HIGH SCHOOL

Yes, it starts that early! If you are lucky enough to know, while you are a student in high school, that you want to become a medical doctor, take the opportunity to get a head start on your preparation for medical school. Take advanced-placement courses, which may enable you to take advanced science courses once you get to college. Get experience with medicine now that will help you decide if medicine is for you and, should you decide that it is, will help you get into medical school. Get a summer job with your family physician or volunteer at a local hospital or nursing home. If you decide medicine is in your future, try to continue this activity once you're in college.

> "Be sure you want to do medicine before you start medical school. Don't just talk to students; talk to practicing doctors. Understand what you're getting into."
>
> —Dr. Darshak M. Sanghavi, former medical student, Johns Hopkins University School of Medicine

Begin Researching Medical Schools

While you are a high school student, you can also begin researching medical schools and checking admission requirements and how to meet them—get your first copy of *Medical School Admission Requirements* (MSAR) now! (For more on this valuable resource, see Chapter 3.) You can order this volume from the Association of American Medical Colleges (AAMC; Web site: http://www.aamc.org). You should also call schools to speak with premed program advisers and, perhaps, make an appointment with a premed or admission counselor at a local university. This will give you inside information on the kind of preparation you will need to succeed in a premed program. It's also good experience for you in presenting yourself to a professional as a mature and motivated student. Formal interviews are uncommon for admission to undergraduate programs, but you can treat this meeting as a practice interview. Try to look your best, and come to your meeting prepared with questions for the college representative as well as information about yourself. Practice sounding confident about your plans for the future, and, if you aren't sure you're going to ace your AP chemistry course, there's no need to mention this. Find out through this meeting and by checking the admission requirements for various schools what the ideal academic program would be, and then follow that program.

You also will decide on your undergraduate school while in high school, and if medical school is in your plans, you may want to choose a college with a good premed program and a good premed adviser. It's a very good idea to speak with premed advisers at the schools you are considering to see how helpful they will be and how extensive their knowledge of medical school admission is. Find out how many premed students the school has and what their rates of acceptance into medical school are before you decide where to attend. Financial considerations may lead you to apply to your state school, but if your grades and SAT scores are such that you may be accepted at more selective universities, apply to those as well. Medical schools consider how difficult your undergraduate school was, and you may just get a better education.

Choosing an Undergraduate School

You should consider not only your medical school future when selecting your undergraduate school; there is, after all, the definite possibility that you will decide not to pursue medical school. You want a school that will suit your learning needs, and you should consider the school's class sizes, location (do you need to be close to family?), overall course offerings (in case you decide Greek, and not medicine, is your true passion), and cost. If you are considering attending a two-year college first, you may want to reconsider: many medical schools do not include community college grades when calculating GPAs; this would require that your prerequisites be taken at a four-year institution (otherwise you could officially have no science GPA). Even if the medical schools to which you apply do accept your two-year-college science courses, they will likely consider the two-year courses less strenuous than those at most four-year colleges, and this will hurt your chances of acceptance. This does not mean you cannot get into medical school if you start your college career at a community college—only that there may be additional factors for you to consider when planning to apply to medical school.

In the long run, it is much more important that you find the school that will be best for you and where you can obtain the best education. Do not limit yourself to attending the school you think will give you the best chance of attending medical school. There are many variables that go into your medical school applications, and your undergraduate institution is just one of them. If you choose your undergraduate school based solely on the school's rate of medical school acceptance but find that the school is too large or too far from home, you may not do well, and this may hurt you more than attending your less competitive state university.

Combined Programs

Some schools offer combined programs that allow you to obtain your bachelor's degree with the assumption that if you do well in your undergraduate studies, you will be admitted to a medical school program upon graduating. Not all of these programs combine the bachelor's degree and M.D. at the same school; some medical schools have joint programs that begin at another university, and others begin in the undergraduate division of the medical school. A few programs are limited to state residents (the City the University of New York, the University of Illinois at Chicago, the State University of New York Health Science Center at Syracuse, and Texas A&M), and though the majority require a full eight years for the completion of the bachelor's degree and M.D., a number of schools reduce the full time for both degrees to six or seven years. Additional information on combined programs may be found in Chapter 3; the MSAR also includes a section on such programs.

PLANNING IN COLLEGE

Do you have to think about medical school from day one? If you've known you want to go to medical school for some time, you should have been planning for medical school before college. If you weren't sure and now you are, or even if medical school remains one of several possibilities for your future, by all means start planning as soon as possible in college. Perhaps you have already spoken to the premed counselor at your college—it may have been part of the school selection process for you. If not, make an appointment with a counselor at his or her earliest convenience, and get their advice on the courses you should be taking in your first year to meet medical school admission requirements.

Premedical Counseling

Your premed adviser may be a member of your college's science faculty or should at least have an interest in those areas. He or she will likely have useful information about the variety of courses offered in your school's chemistry department, for example, and can recommend the one that will be best for you. The best premed advisers will have advice and guidance for you during every step of your undergraduate career and will guide you through the medical school admission process. They may even be able to advise you about possible volunteer or internship opportunities in health-related fields. However, not all counselors will be well informed and helpful, nor will they necessarily have a lot of time to spend advising you. At the very least, your adviser should have information on medical school admission requirements and important deadlines during the application process. At many schools, the premedical adviser does not routinely meet with premedical students until their sophomore year. If this is the case, you will need to do more planning independently.

Helping Your Premedical Counselor Help You

If you are fortunate enough to have a wonderfully knowledgeable and helpful premed adviser, take full advantage of him or her and develop a good relationship. Schedule meetings and be punctual. If he or she requires that you meet with them once each semester, you might want to make the extra effort to meet with them a few more times. Bring copies of materials you wish to share, such as papers, tests, and medical school information. Your adviser will build a file on you using this and other material. You must be honest with him or her about your career goals and your academic successes and failures. The better your adviser knows you, the better recommendation he or she will be able to write for you when the time comes. If the adviser knows that you received a C in organic chemistry the semester your father was hospitalized, he or she can use this personal information in the letter to explain why you remain a good medical school candidate despite that C.

"My premed advisor stressed me out and told me to do more premed things (I was a sociology major)—advice I ignored, and it hurt me."

—medical student, Yale University School of Medicine

Do not be dishonest with your adviser. He or she will likely find out the truth and will be aware of your grades and Medical College Admission Test (MCAT) scores. If an adviser feels that you have been dishonest, he or she may find you lacking integrity and will write a letter of recommendation for you that is mediocre at best. This can seriously compromise your chances of admission into medical school.

Your premed adviser may tell you that your grades or MCAT scores are not competitive enough and may even discourage you from applying to medical school. What do you do if this happens? It's up to you, of course. If you feel strongly about medical school, you can complete your research and apply without the assistance of your college's premed office. This will be difficult, and the lack of a recommendation letter from you premed adviser may leave a glaring hole in your application file. On the other hand, perhaps your school is known to have an unhelpful premed system. In any case, apply if you are compelled to do so, but if your adviser and others think you are unlikely to be accepted, be realistic enough to have a fallback plan in case you are not accepted.

Ask your counselor every question you have, and have them put you in touch with other premed students. Perhaps your university sponsors a premed student group, but if there is no such formal alliance, you can still contact other premed students on campus. Those in your class can offer support and act as study partners during exam time; sophomores, juniors, and seniors can share their knowledge and research about advanced courses and medical schools, as well as stories of their experiences with difficult professors and the MCAT.

If your adviser is accessible and helpful, sometime before your senior year he or she may help you make a list of the dozen or so schools to which you will apply. Have the adviser read your application essay, and let him or her know which schools accept or reject you. If all goes well, you can write a thank you note when you begin your first year at Harvard Medical School.

> [My premed adviser] wrote an excellent recommendation letter and helped organize my applications."
>
> —Dr. Darshak M. Sanghavi, former medical student, Johns Hopkins University School of Medicine

ADMISSION REQUIREMENTS

Get familiar with medical school admission requirements and deadlines as soon as possible. You can begin by perusing the MSAR in high school for information on the 125 allopathic medical schools in the U.S. By all means, you should see if your college premed adviser has a copy of this volume to help you plan your courses. The *College Information Booklet*, available from the American Association of Colleges of Osteopathic Medicine (AACOM; Web site: http://www. aacom.org), gives similar information on the nineteen U.S. osteopathic medical schools. Armed with information on requirements and deadlines, you can plan your academic career accordingly. It is likely that you will take the MCAT in April of your junior year, and by the time you take it, you really should have had one year each of general and organic chemistry, biology, and physics. Courses in biology, general and organic chemistry, and physics are required for admission to most medical schools; according to the MSAR, in 1998, 109 of the 125 U.S. medical schools required physics, 108 required organic chemistry, and 107 required general chemistry. Many schools also require English, and some require calculus and other courses as well.

Science Courses

At most undergraduate schools, you will have a few options when you decide which courses to take to meet the admission requirements of medical schools. There is usually an organic chemistry course offered for chemistry majors, as well as one for everyone else. You should take the courses offered for majors, because these are the most difficult; medical schools expect you to take the more difficult course, and in fact, the course for majors may be more helpful to you when the MCAT rolls around. However, if you don't think you have the time and energy to devote to organic chemistry for chemistry majors—it is likely to be grueling—you might want to opt for the nonscience major sequence so that you don't ruin your entire GPA while struggling through this course. Medical school admission committees really have no way of knowing that the course you took was or was not the more difficult one offered. This is not to encourage you to take the easiest courses possible in order to pad your GPA. "Physics for Poets" is not likely to give you the background you will need to succeed on the MCAT and in medical school, and if you are the kind of person who looks for the easy way out, perhaps you should not go into medicine. Whichever courses you decide upon, research the instructor; if different sections are offered by different instructors, find out who is the best teacher (or whose teaching style best suits your learning style) by talking to former students and to your adviser.

You will likely, as most students do, take general chemistry in your freshman year, along with a lower-level biology course. In your sophomore year, you might want to take organic chemistry, along with more biology. As a junior, you can take your yearlong physics course, which will complete your major prerequisites. If the schools to which you plan to apply have other requirements, such as math or English, you can take these along the way or leave them for your senior year after you have the MCAT out of the way. While taking these prerequisites, you will also need to fulfill the requirements for your major as well as any distribution requirements your college may have.

Other Courses

Medical schools look for well-rounded students, so even if you decide that you will be a chemistry or biology major, take courses in other topics of interest to you—English, a foreign language, philosophy, or history. In addition to making you a more well-rounded person, if you love history, you may love the work for your history courses, which might alleviate the drudgery of studying for advanced chemistry. If you decide to take the opportunity to study abroad for a year, good for you—this can be a very rewarding and enriching experience. Keep your schedule for medical school admission in mind, however, and plan to have your prerequisites out of the way in time for the MCAT (and to be in the U.S. for the MCAT). It may be unwise to take required courses while abroad; the grades may not be accepted by U.S. colleges, and you may have a hard time with an organic chemistry class conducted in French, even if you speak the language well before you go to France. Perhaps this means your study abroad will be in your senior year; this means that your application materials should be completed before you depart, and you should make yourself available for interviews in the U.S., which can be a costly necessity.

Your Major

Once in college, should you major in one of the sciences? The answer to this question depends mainly on your interests. As a premed student, you will need to take many science courses, and if it looks to you like these courses will only fit into your four years of college if you major in biology or chemistry, then perhaps you should do so. If, however, you have room for these courses in addition to a major (while meeting all of your college's graduation requirements) and you have a love of European history or Spanish literature, you should strongly consider majoring in the area that truly interests you. If you major in something you really like, perhaps you'll enjoy the work you do for those courses so much that it will help you get through the labs and exams you have in biochemistry and help keep your GPA high. Certainly medical schools are looking for interesting and well-rounded students, and your nonscience major may help you distinguish yourself in your application and interview. You may also find your Spanish major helpful later on, if you do your residency in an urban area or an area with a large Spanish-speaking population. Majoring outside the sciences will not necessarily hurt your chance of admission into medical school, although most students applying to medical school do major in the sciences. If you major in the social sciences or fine arts and still do well in your science courses and on the MCAT, you will look very good to medical school admission officers. Don't assume that majoring in biology is your best bet for medical school admission, but if you happen to love biology, choose it as your major. You can always minor in Spanish literature. Remember that medical schools are highly selective these days; there are many more applicants than there are spaces, and if you aren't accepted into medical school, you may need to use your major to plan another career.

According to the 2000–2001 MSAR, 46.6 percent of applicants for the 1998–99 year majored in the biological sciences; 39.9 percent of those applicants were accepted. Only 12.6 percent of the applicants for that year majored in nonscience subjects, but 45.5 percent of those applicants were accepted. These numbers indicate that majoring in history or a foreign language will not hurt your chances of acceptance into medical school (in fact, 53.5 percent of those history majors who applied were accepted into medical school, the highest rate of acceptance for that year). The nonscience majors still had to meet admission requirements and were undoubtedly well-qualified applicants. Whatever major you choose, plan to work hard and do your best.

> "Figure out what distinguishes you and work on it. It's easier to distinguish yourself by doing something different than by outstudying your peers."
>
> —former medical student, University of Texas Southwestern Medical Center at Dallas

Extracurricular Activities

As mentioned earlier, medical school admission officers are looking for well-rounded students to enter their programs. Are you such a candidate? If you are, then you're a step ahead. If not, what can you do to make yourself a better candidate?

In addition to taking courses outside the sciences to broaden your experience, remember to get involved with extracurricular activities. Though not required by medical schools, you will find that they help you get into medical school, as your high school activities likely helped you get into college. Those that present you as a good candidate for medical school are best; volunteer at your local hospital or nursing home, or, if you have the specific interest, volunteer in the pediatrics ward of the hospital, in a chronic care facility, or with your local emergency medical services team. You can find opportunities such as these by calling area hospitals and nursing homes, hospices, and other chronic care facilities. Volunteers are usually needed and welcome in such organizations, and the experience may change the course of your future career—you may decide that pediatrics or emergency medicine is the work that will matter in your life. Call and arrange a meeting with a facility that interests you and then get started.

You may also gain experience by volunteering as an assistant on a faculty member's science research project or by applying for a summer research fellowship. This will not allow you hands-on experience with patients, and so may not be the best experience for you unless you are interested in a research career or a joint M.D./ Ph.D. program. Research is part of medical school, however, and this is a good addition to your resume. Such experiences may put you into contact with doctors and others who may have valuable advice to offer—someone you volunteer for would also be a good person to write a recommendation for you when you apply to medical school. In addition, activities in health-related fields will not only demonstrate your interest in medicine, but will give you the opportunity to work in a medical environment and see if it really is for you.

Activities outside the sciences will continue to make you look like a well-rounded person. If you love Spanish, join the Spanish club or live in the foreign language dorm. If you have the time, get a job in the library, join the soccer or tennis team, be a resident assistant, become a teaching assistant, or tutor. Don't overextend yourself, though, and remember that it is most important for you to maintain your GPA and, eventually, do well on the MCAT.

> "Spend time in a hospital or a doctor's office or both."
> —medical student, Yale University School of Medicine

What GPA Is Required by Medical Schools?

As you look through the MSAR, you will find that it is full of valuable information. One of the things it tells you about each medical school is the selection factors each school uses to determine who they accept. Some schools provide information on the latest accepted class at the time of publication (for the 2000–2001 MSAR, this data is for the class entering in 1998), including average GPA and MCAT scores and the percentage of applicants accepted. (Many schools do not offer this specific information, in which case your premed adviser should have an idea of their acceptance criteria.) Some schools will break this information down further, giving information such as average science and nonscience GPA and the percentage of women students. According to the MSAR, in 1998–99, the average undergraduate GPA for accepted applicants was 3.57. Only .5 percent had a GPA of 2.5 or less, and for those whose GPA was 3.0, a noticeable improvement in their academic performance was evident in their later years of college. A simple guideline to follow is that a mean GPA of 3.5 should be attempted. If, on average, accepted students have a 3.5 GPA, then many students will have a GPA above 3.5, and many will be below 3.3. You should at least try for the mean, however, to better you chances for acceptance.

Science GPA

Schools will look at your science GPA separately. This does not mean that you must have straight A grades in your science courses, but it certainly does mean that you cannot get C and D grades in your science courses and then pull up your overall GPA with A grades in easy electives. Poor grades in the required science courses will definitely hurt your chances of admission to medical school. Where you went to school and what you did there will be factored in when medical schools consider your science and overall GPAs. If you can keep a 3.5 and still participate in extracurricular activities or hold a job, that's great. If trying for a 3.7 pulls you away from those outside activities, you should probably be satisfied with your 3.5 and stay involved in your other pursuits. If you're working really hard and a 3.3 is the best you can do, then it's the best you can do. Perhaps you will stand out in other ways for the medical school admission officers. If a 3.0 GPA was your best but you held down a part-time job and volunteered at a nursing home or went to Harvard, admission committees will consider your 3.0 differently than that of a student who attended a noncompetitive state university and had few or no activities. Also, if your GPA is not stellar, how well you do on the MCAT becomes much more important.

Standardized Testing (MCAT)

The Medical College Admission Test (MCAT) is the standardized test you are required to take at least once in order to gain admission to medical school. The test is weighted differently by each medical school, but it is safe to say that your MCAT scores are a crucial element in your application, and you will want to be well prepared for this exam. The MCAT is considered a good predictor of your medical school performance as well as your performance on the U.S. Medical Licensing Examinations (USMLE) medical boards. Because the test is standardized, your scores are considered with the same weight as those of students from different backgrounds and schools. The test is an objective method of comparison between all applicants—the competitiveness of your college or the courses you took will have no effect on how the scores are viewed by the admission committee. The MCAT is offered on one Saturday in April and one Saturday in August of each year (the AAMC makes provisions for a Sunday test if religious requirements or other conflicts intervene; the student is charged an additional $10 fee for these arrangements).

When to Take the MCAT

You should plan on taking this test in April of your junior year in college. If you are exceptionally well prepared, you may want to take the test in August prior to your junior year; if you do not do as well as expected, you may retake the test in April or the following August. Most medical schools prefer that applicants take the MCAT in April because of the short period between the August test date and most application deadlines. MCAT scores are usually available approximately sixty days after your test date. If your application file is complete except for your MCAT scores, processing of your application will be delayed until your scores are received. If you take the test for the first time in August prior to your senior year and you do not do well, you are stuck with those scores—medical schools will be making their admission decisions before you have the opportunity to better your scores. (If you are applying to an early decision plan, you must take the MCAT in April of your junior year.) If you have the MCAT out of the way in April, you can relax and work on the rest of your application, but if you do not take the MCAT until August, your other initial application materials will be due before you take the test, creating a hectic summer for you before your senior year. To make things easier on yourself, plan to take the MCAT in April of your junior year.

The dates for the MCAT in 2000 are April 15 (registration deadline: March 10) and August 19 (registration deadline: July 14). The fee for the MCAT in 2000 is $165. If you are unable to pay this fee, a fee-reduction program is available that reduces the fee to $60. An application must be filed for the fee reduction; for this form and application deadline information, contact your premedical adviser or contact the MCAT Program Office (telephone: 319-337-1357). You may obtain a registration packet through your adviser or by calling the MCAT Program Office (packets are available in January of each year). The Association of American Medical Colleges also has this information available; you can download the form from their Web site (http://www.aamc.org) or call them (202-828-0600).

A note for minority students   Minority students can opt to participate in the AAMC's Medical Minority Applicant Registry (Med-MAR) when they take their MCAT. Any medical school applicant who is a member of a minority group that is underrepresented in medicine (African Americans, Native Americans, Mexican Americans, and mainland Puerto Ricans) can have their biographical information and MCAT scores sent to minority affairs and admission offices of all U.S. medical schools free of charge through Med-MAR. Medical school officers can then contact students directly for more information. If you want to know more about Med-MAR, go to the AAMC Web site listed above.

What's on the Test?

The MCAT is a four-part test that resembles the SAT in format. The four sections are verbal reasoning, physical sciences, biological sciences, and a writing sample. You will be tested on your scientific knowledge as well as on your problem-solving and writing skills. Each of the first three parts is worth a maximum of 15 points (and a minimum of 1 point). The writing sample is scored differently; you may receive a letter grade in the range of J, which is the lowest, to T, which is the highest. The highest possible score on the MCAT, therefore, is a 45. You will have 5¾ hours to complete the test, with timed allotments for each section (the test takes over seven hours, including the rest breaks). The three numerically scored sections are multiple-choice, with four choices for each section. If you've never taken a multiple-choice test of this kind, you will certainly want to take a few practice exams to prepare yourself for the format. You will have two parts of the test in the morning, followed by a lunch break. After lunch, you will take the final two parts of the test.

Verbal reasoning   This is the first section you will have on your test date. You will have 85 minutes for this section, followed by a 10-minute break. This section includes sixty-five multiple choice questions that will test your reading comprehension abilities. Nine to ten prose sections of 500 to 600 words are taken from the humanities, social sciences, and natural sciences. Following each passage is a series of six to ten questions relating to that passage. All questions can be answered by evaluating the passage.

Physical sciences   You will have this section second, and will have 100 minutes to complete all of the questions, after which you are given a 60-minute lunch break. The physical sciences section includes seventy-seven multiple-choice questions on physics and general chemistry. Ten to eleven passages of 250 words are followed by groups of four to eight questions relating to that passage; fifteen additional questions are independent of any written passages.

To do well on this section, you must be able to read and comprehend information in graphs and tables, you should understand trends and tendencies in such information, and you should be able to identify the best way to present data. The passages you read may be complex, but the questions accompanying the passages will test you on basic principles you will have learned in your college courses.

Writing sample   This is the essay portion of the exam, and it is your first section following the lunch break. You will have 60 minutes to compose two essays (30 minutes per essay) on topics presented in this section. You do not get to choose your topic, and you cannot prepare your essay beforehand. The topics will not be related to the other sections of the test, nor will they have to do with the medical school application process. Again, in looking for balanced applicants, medical schools want to know that you are not only proficient in the sciences, but that you are also a good communicator. The writing sample questions are composed of a statement followed by three writing tasks. This section is followed by a 10-minute break.

Biological sciences   The final test section is allotted 100 minutes, and like the physical sciences section, includes seventy-seven multiple-choice questions. Biology and organic chemistry are covered in this section; sixty-two questions in sets of four to eight questions follow ten or eleven 250-word passages, and fifteen questions are independent of such passages. Again, you will need to be able to comprehend information in graphs, tables, and figures. Memorization is not the most important thing for this section; your understanding of basic concepts, vocabulary, constants, and equations will be tested.

How Is the MCAT Scored?

Your number of correct answers for the numerically scored sections will be turned into a scaled score and percentile based on the scores of others who took the test when you did. Each essay in your writing sample will be scored by two readers; all four scores are combined to create your letter score. The current version of the MCAT was introduced in 1991, and your scores can be no older than that. Some schools require that your MCAT scores be much more recent; check admission requirements in the MSAR or with individual medical schools for information on MCAT requirements.

How Important Are High Marks?

It is very important that you do well on the MCAT if you want to be a successful candidate for medical school admission. Be sure to look through the MSAR for an indication of how various schools use MCAT scores and what the scores were for accepted applicants. Remember that medical schools may list the average for accepted applicants, which means that if 10 was the average, many students scored above or below a 10. Generally, a score of 10 or higher on the first three sections and a Q on the essay portion are considered quite good. The average for applicants is closer to an 8 for numerically scored sections and an N for the writing sample. You should aim for scores of 10 or 11, and note that the most competitive schools will be looking for scores of 12 or higher. (Osteopathic medical schools tend to accept students with slightly lower MCAT scores, on average, than do allopathic schools.) If your scores are below a 10 on the three numerically scored sections, it's in your best interest to take the MCAT a second time. Remember that even if you get straight 10s on the MCAT, if the rest of your application indicates that you are a below-average student, the MCAT alone will not be enough to get you into medical school. If your GPA is borderline, however, stellar MCAT scores may be what push you over the mark for a particular school. Whatever your particular overall situation, try your best to do well on the MCAT, and leave yourself time to retake the test if necessary.

Studying for the MCAT

The importance of your note-taking skills will finally be realized as you study for the MCAT, which you really must do. By the time you take the MCAT, you should have fulfilled the medical school admission course requirements, which will provide you with the course background you need for the test. Your premedical adviser should be able to tell you how premed students from your college have fared on the MCAT in previous years; this may be an indicator of how well your college's science courses prepare students for the MCAT. Of course, it is possible that earlier students did not study as hard as you did for those courses, but if most of the earlier premed students at your school received scores of 8 on the three scored sections, you may want to supplement your science knowledge before you take the MCAT. There are numerous study aids available for the MCAT, including Peterson's *The Gold Standard MCAT*. Preparatory courses are also available that might help you study for the MCAT. Courses, while helpful, can be prohibitively expensive; if you're on a budget, buy a few MCAT study guides and arrange for a study group with your fellow premed students.

Be sure to prepare for all parts of the MCAT; do not ignore those parts for which you feel well prepared, and do not only study for the subjects in which you excel. You must do well on all parts of the MCAT; do not think that your 12 in physical sciences will compensate for a 7 in biological sciences (or verbal reasoning). As with all other parts of your application, your MCAT scores must present you as a well-rounded student whose writing abilities and verbal comprehension match your scientific knowledge.

Collect all of your science notes. If you were a hyperorganized student with very good attendance, you will have coherent and complete notes, which are essential study aids for you when preparing for the MCAT. If you're reading this book as a high school student or in your first year of college, please heed this advice: *take excellent and complete notes for all of your courses.* Attend classes regularly, pay close attention, and take complete notes that you will be able to understand for this week's quiz, for the course final, and two to three years later when you are studying for the MCAT. If you take notes faithfully but they are illegible, they will be of little use, and if you attend class irregularly and take very good notes once a week, that will not help you either. Do not rely on your powerful memory; you may be surprised at how little you recall after a year or more of many other courses.

Keep your notes for each course separate from other courses and date your notes each day, whether you use a loose-leaf binder or spiral-bound notebook. If you aren't sure how to take thorough notes, see if your college offers a seminar on note-taking for college—many do, and it can be a much different experience taking notes for college than it was in high school. If you think you're taking good notes but you aren't sure, compare your notes with other students in your classes—you and they may benefit from the experience. You may find it difficult to keep up with your professor, in which case developing your own shorthand may be helpful. If you find that your handwriting suffers as you write quickly in class, you might want to try rewriting your notes after class. This will not only help you to have better notes, but it can be a powerful tool for you in reviewing the class materials each day. Perhaps other note-taking tools will work for you: different colored pens, index cards, a particular size or style of notebooks. Generally, the more simple your note-taking materials, the better. The less you have to think about which color or card to use, the more you can simply focus on your class and taking thorough notes. You may need to experiment at first, but it's important that you focus on developing your note-taking skills. Find what works for you and then take notes!

In addition to your course notes, you should keep all textbooks and supplementary materials, such as handouts, lab books, papers, quizzes, and exams; these will also be of great help to you as you study for the MCAT.

You can study wherever you feel most comfortable: in your dorm or your dorm's common room, in the library, in a local coffeehouse, or in some other location. You may find it easier to study with a group of students, and it is a good idea to set up a regular study session with other students who plan to take the MCAT; however you should also plan to do a good deal of studying on your own. Study for the MCAT much as you would for any exam—by reviewing the material until it is familiar to you. Unlike most of your college exams, the MCAT gives you the advantage of practice exams (perhaps you were lucky enough to have had practice exams from earlier semesters to help you with your course work; this will be a familiar method of study for you). You should use practice exams from your earliest study time rather than waiting until you feel confident with the material. That way, by completely reviewing each exam, you can gauge your progress as you do better on each practice exam you take. Follow time specifications for the practice exams (and don't use a calculator) to make the practice exams more realistic.

The periodic table and some equations and constants are provided in the exam, but you must know a certain amount of math for the MCAT. A calculator may not be taken to the exam, so if you are dependent on yours, practice the old-fashioned methods you learned long ago for performing basic arithmetic (addition, subtraction, multiplication, and division), proportions, percentages, ratios, and square roots. Be familiar with metric units, and be able to convert metric and imperial units. Know how to balance equations and understand logarithms, scientific notation, quadratic and simultaneous equations, graphs, and basic algebra. Be able to calculate an arithmetic mean and determine the range for a set of data. Understand the basics of statistics and be able to calculate mathematical probability. Understand basic trigonometry, the concept of experimental error, and vector additions and subtractions. You do not need to know statistics.

This may seem like a lot, but most of this mathematical knowledge is basic, and if you are rusty in some areas, preparatory test books can help you brush up on your math. Time will be of the essence when you are taking the MCAT, so you must be able to perform simple mathematical functions quickly. Review until you are comfortable with the required math, but do not use a calculator while studying for the MCAT; increasing your reliance on a calculator will hurt you when you get to the test and must do all of the calculations on paper.

Use the other methods you have learned in studying for your exams to learn the necessary theorems and equations: use flash cards, have a friend quiz you, and create mnemonics to help you memorize material. By the time you are studying for the MCAT, you will have done well in college for several years and should know what kinds of study methods you require. The MCAT should be studied for in the way that works best for you, though it is a much lengthier and more comprehensive test than your previous exams. You should try to do at least one practice exam that follows the MCAT format to gauge the stamina you will need for a full day of testing.

Remember that studying for the MCAT is a process for which you must be motivated. If you have done well in your courses (which you must do to get into medical school), it should not be difficult for you to recall or relearn this material. If you find that your courses have inadequately prepared you, you will need more time to prepare for the MCAT. Try to assess this early, and do not expect, whatever your course preparation, to be able to study for the MCAT in the week before you take the test. If you give yourself plenty of time to study for the test, you will have time to keep up with your courses (which you must do if you are taking the MCAT in April of your junior year) and with your extracurricular activities. Your outside activities remain important not only because they are necessary for your complete application, but also because they can provide you with a much needed outlet during the stressful weeks preceding the MCAT. There is such a thing as studying too much—keep to a study schedule and allot time for breaks.

Test Day

The night before the test, you should not stay up all night cramming for the exam, but rather get a good night's sleep to prepare for the long day ahead. Pack a healthy (but not too heavy) lunch and snacks, if you think you'll need them to keep your energy up, and on the morning of the exam, eat a good breakfast. Once you begin the test, be sure to answer all of the multiple-choice questions, because an unanswered question is the same as an incorrectly answered question. If you do not know the answers to some questions, make your best educated guess. Pace yourself and don't waste a lot of time on a single question—answer those you know, and then go back to those you skipped. Guess if you don't know the answer. Read the questions carefully and feel free to make notes while figuring out your answers; they may help you come to the correct solution. If you find you are running out of time, skip the passages and go directly to the questions, and then go back and read the passage with the questions in mind. Stay focused during the rest and lunch breaks: relax and have a snack, but don't obsess over how well or poorly you think you've done or how well others might be doing, and don't try to do more cramming for the afternoon session.

You now know the requirements for most medical schools, have made a list of the courses and activities you will take to make yourself a better medical school candidate, and have taken the MCAT. Where should you apply? We tackle this subject in the next chapter.

Chapter 3

Selecting a Medical School

WHERE TO START

How do you begin your search for the right medical school? You should rely on the MSAR for basic information, but by all means ask your college premed adviser for help in identifying schools whose requirements you meet. Your premed peers, particularly those who are already applying to medical schools, can offer you inside information on the schools to which they have applied as well as any they may have visited. Another great source of information for you will be current medical students and alumni from those schools in which you are interested. Perhaps a student from your university now attends the University of Michigan Medical School, which you are also considering. Ask your premed adviser if he or she can put you in touch with that student, whose inside view of the program and the application process can be invaluable to you.

Guidebooks

Medical school guidebooks may be helpful; Peterson's publishes *U.S. and Canadian Medical Schools: A Comprehensive Guide to All 159 Accredited Medical Schools* and *The Insider's Guide to Medical Schools: Medical Students Tell You What You Really Want to Know*. This volume is particularly useful because it presents general information on U.S. medical schools, compiled by Peterson's, as well as specific information, including sections on admission and financial aid, the preclinical and clinical years, and social life and a bottom-line summary of each school—all written by a current medical student at that school.

While this book will give you only one student's view of a particular school, it is a good place to start; where else can you look to find out that students at the University of South Dakota Medical School organize an annual ski trip to the Black Hills or that Madison, Wisconsin, has been nicknamed "Mad Town" because of the rowdy University of Wisconsin campus? With these volumes, your copy of *Medical School Admission Requirements* (MSAR), and the advice of your adviser and peers, you should be able to begin making a list of schools that interest you, and then you can make your search more detailed.

IDENTIFYING SCHOOLS AND CRITERIA

When choosing the medical schools to which you should apply, many of the factors you considered when you selected your undergraduate institution will again come into play. You must consider the size, cost, and location of the school as well as the quality of medical education and medical specialties the school offers. If you prefer a smaller class size, note that the University of Illinois at Chicago School of Medicine had 286 students in the 1998–99 entering class. For the same year, Northeastern Ohio University's College of Medicine had 25 new students, and Morehouse School of Medicine in Georgia had 34 new students. If you are very uncomfortable in an urban environment, you may not wish to apply to Columbia University College of Physicians and Surgeons; if you are extremely concerned about finances, you may not want to apply as an out-of-state student to the University of Colorado School of Medicine, where nonresident tuition and fees were $55,471 for 1998–99, making it the most expensive medical school option in the U.S.

You can determine a great deal about a school from the MSAR and other guides, as well as from your adviser. Your copy of the MSAR should be well worn after you have completed the application process, and it will likely be the best single source of information you will find, because the Association of American Medical Colleges (AAMC) gathers its information directly from the medical schools accredited by the Liaison Committee on Medical Education (LCME). You will use the MSAR to make your initial school lists and, later, to recall deadlines and review before your interviews. The early chapters of the MSAR include information on the application process, and Chapter 11 includes a profile of each U.S. medical school (Chapter 12 profiles the Canadian medical schools). These profiles will help you with your initial medical school research; some of the variables you will want to consider, including the program goals, size, location, and cost, are discussed below.

Catalogs

You should request catalogs from medical schools you're interested in and read them carefully. Remember that catalogs are published by the schools and will not present an unbiased view, but they will include valuable information on deadlines, costs, course offerings, curricula, faculty interests, and so on. You will be able to find out if a school has a high-technology approach, when your clinical training will begin and where it will take place, how many students apply and are accepted to the school, what the estimated cost of attendance is, what financial aid is available, how large a library the school has, and what teaching and recreational facilities the school offers its students.

Use the resources you have gathered to determine which schools are more likely to accept you based on your grades and MCAT scores, your interests, and the school's various attributes. You must first consider entrance requirements at medical schools to find those who will accept a student with your qualifications and background. Look at ratings, such as those by *U.S. News & World Report*, to see which schools are well ranked, but do not let this be of great influence. Look at the history of a school and the programs it has to offer before deciding where you should apply. If you are interested in pediatric medicine, Washington University School of Medicine in St. Louis may be of interest to you because of the school's affiliation with St. Louis Children's Hospital, but note that the 1998 entering class had an average GPA of 3.81 and average MCAT scores of 11.1 on verbal, 12.3 on physical sciences, and 12.4 on biological sciences. You must balance your interests with schools likely to accept you, and if your GPA is a 3.3, Washington University may not be a good choice for your final list. Pennsylvania State University College of Medicine is also affiliated with a children's hospital, and the average GPA for recent applicants was 3.6, with average MCAT scores of 10.

Hospitals and Specialized Programs

Many medical schools have particular areas of research or medical specialties for which they are well known. Some are research oriented, many will be affiliated with university teaching hospitals, and some will be affiliated with other clinical facilities in which you will receive your clinical training. As mentioned in Chapter 1, the hospitals and other facilities with which a medical school is affiliated are quite important, because they determine the type and quality of the clinical training you will receive. This training, in turn, will lead you into your residency "match." (The process by which you are matched to one of the residency positions in the U.S. is complicated and somewhat vague, but in essence, you select your top choices of residencies and are then compared with other students desiring the same residency. The school you attend is important, as are your grades and clinical experience, but just how important each factor is remains mysterious.)

Find out which teaching hospitals the medical school has an affiliation with—there should be more than one. The hospital may specialize in pediatrics or emergency medicine; it may have a community outreach program or a primary medicine focus. If it is a university hospital, it may be more research oriented, and many of the doctors will be affiliated with the university, teaching or supervising medical students in clerkships. A rural county hospital may be a smaller environment, and you may be able to move around more, but there could be a low patient volume and a lack of some of the clinical variety you might find in a larger facility. It is a good idea to look for a school that has not only a teaching hospital, but also nonhospital facilities in which you will be trained. These could include clinics and local medical practices. Also, check into the level of technology practiced at the hospitals affiliated with each school. The importance of technology in medicine cannot be overstressed, and you should look for facilities with up-to-the-minute technology, particularly in the areas that interest you. The latest technical advances will be important not only in the clinical training facilities of a medical school, but also in the medical school curriculum (see the next section).

You want to be well-trained in a variety of areas, and this may not be possible if the medical school will send you to one small facility for all of your clerkships. Mainly, it is important that the clinical teaching facilities focus on areas of medicine that are of interest to you. Do not go where there is no geriatric medicine if that really interests you. Check the MSAR and college catalogs to match your interests with medical schools, and if you need additional information, do not hesitate to contact medical school admission offices with your questions. Once you have your degree, you may decide you do not want to practice medicine after all, but would rather be a professor or a researcher or perhaps you want to enter the administrative side of medicine. If you choose to practice medicine, note that there are many specialties from which you must choose, and the school you attend will in large part determine the experience you get. You may be led to a residency in emergency medicine because of your clinical training in an emergency medicine facility, but if you enter medical school with an interest in surgery or public health, be sure that you will be able to obtain clinical experience in that area at your medical school.

Curriculum

Your four years of study were discussed in depth in Chapter 1 but should be mentioned again here, because the medical school curriculum is something you should consider when deciding where you will apply. Be knowledgeable about the courses you will be required to take and the teaching methods employed by the schools you are considering. As mentioned above, the types of clerkship available to you will matter a great deal in the long run because they will provide you with your clinical experience, and this is how you will not only select a specialty, but also become a good candidate for a residency in that area of specialty. If you studied surgery in your course work but were never able to do a clerkship in surgery or arrange a surgery internship, you will be very unlikely to match into one of the highly coveted surgical residencies available around the country.

The skills you are able to obtain, both in your clerkships and your course work, should be up-to-date; in large part, this means checking into the technology available at a given medical school and its affiliated clinical facilities. Do they use computer-based diagnostic programs? Do medical students have access to online resources and databases? Does the school offer clerkships in any computer science and medicine fields? Even if you are not particularly interested in the latest technology, you will find it important to your success as a medical student and doctor that you embrace new technology and be willing to learn to use it. If your medical school is decades behind in medical technological innovations, you may not receive the training you will need to become a competent physician.

In addition to the areas of medicine you will study in your clerkships, you should consider how many clerkships are required at each medical school. If the school requires nothing beyond the five core clerkships (medicine, obstetrics/gynecology, pediatrics, psychiatry, and surgery), they may not have the variety you are looking for, and you may not get enough clinical experience to decide what your specialty should be. Usually, a certain number of core clerkship are required, and these are followed in your final year by a number of elective clerkships. If the medical school has a variety of teaching facilities, you should be allowed the freedom to create the elective clerkships in which you are interested. If the medical school catalog does not indicate what these electives are, contact the medical school for specific information.

> "Coming into medical school, I was intent on becoming a surgeon. My view of surgeons, even through the beginning of medical school, was based on books and television. I thought of these hot shots that saved lives every day and knew everything. When I finally did surgery as a medical student, however, I found that it was quite tedious. I enjoyed seeing the cases the first or second time, but beyond that I found it boring. I have a short attention span and need constant stimulation to keep my focus. So that's why I decided on emergency medicine. You really don't know what you're going to face the next minute let alone the next day."
>
> —Dr. Sachin Shah, former medical student, Villanova–MCP Hahnemann University accelerated program

Cost

The cost of attending medical school is staggering and should be a factor you consider when selecting the medical school to which you will apply. Boston University, with 1998–99 annual tuition and fees of $34,700 for all students, is the second most expensive medical school in the U.S. If you are a resident of North Carolina, however, you could have attended the East Carolina University School of Medicine for the 1998–99 tuition of $2,132 or the University of North Carolina at Chapel Hill for $2,502. Georgia residents paid only $5,345 in tuition and fees for 1998–99 to attend the Medical College of Georgia School of Medicine.

All students should apply to their state university because in-state acceptance rates are usually quite good and because in-state tuition and fees are much lower than for out-of-state students, as you will find when applying to state universities outside your home state. At the University of Colorado, which is the most expensive medical school for out-of-state students, in-state students paid $13,094 for the 1998–99 academic year. At the University of Alabama School of Medicine, for example, in-state tuition and fees were $9,348 in 1998–99, whereas out-of-state students paid $22,942 in tuition and fees each year. At the same school for the 1998–99 year, 165 applicants were accepted from a pool of 1,711 students; that's an acceptance rate of less than 10 percent. Of those accepted students, 150 were in-state applicants, who comprised only 501 of the entire applicant pool. In-state students had a nearly 30 percent acceptance rate, as opposed to a 1.2 percent acceptance rate for out-of-state students applying to the University of Alabama. Not all state universities accept so few out-of-state applicants, but you will find that a bias toward in-state students at state universities is the norm. Do not be fooled into thinking that because it is a state school, your state university will not afford you a good education. You do not always get what you pay for; in the latest *U.S. News & World Report* rankings, six of the top twenty medical schools are state universities.

Cost should not be the most important factor you consider in deciding where to apply, but it will likely be a factor, because you will have to finance your medical school education, largely through student loans. For information on estimating costs, budgeting, and financial aid, see Chapter 5. In addition to the cost of tuition, you will have to consider your cost of living, which is directly related to the location of the medical school.

Location

Where a school is located will undoubtedly affect your decision to apply (or not to apply). This does not mean that geography should be the deciding factor in the school selection process, but this element should not be ignored. Should you be willing to go anyplace at all that might accept you? Should you limit your applications to a particular geographic region, such as New England? Both of these are extreme possibilities, and your use of location should probably fall somewhere in the middle of the two. You should consider those schools outside your dream location if they are more likely to accept you (apply to schools outside New York or Hawaii, for example), but also know your preferences and limitations and make concessions to them. If you are a country person who has never spent any time in an urban area, at least visit a few big-city schools, and perhaps apply to those that won't put you into culture shock; Indiana University School of Medicine in Indianapolis may be a better choice than Mount Sinai School of Medicine of the City University of New York. In the same way, a New Yorker may be miserable at the University of Mississippi School of Medicine in Jackson.

Again, you should consider schools in areas that are unfamiliar to you before deciding where to apply; the city-dweller may discover a love of small-town life, and the country-dweller may love the pace of a large city, but don't apply blindly. Do your research on the schools first, and if you find a few on your list whose locations make you uncertain, try to arrange a visit to that school prior to application time. This will make you more certain of the applications you file and will also help you at application time, because you will know a bit more about the school than the average candidate. Try to see the campus and the surrounding town and set up a meeting with someone in the admission department for a tour. (Tours are nearly always led by students at the school who are chosen because they will represent the school well and present it as a good place to be; their input will not necessarily be the insider information you need to make your decision, but they may be helpful just the same.)

Cost of Living

In addition to questions of urban and rural locations, there are issues such as cost of living, which is high in most major metropolitan areas; crime and safety; and transportation, both to school and to visit family and friends during breaks. The culture and social life available to you may be important (though you may have little free time to enjoy them), as may the kind of outdoor activities accessible to the campus; if swimming, hiking, and camping are essential to your well-being and offer you great stress relief, you may want a medical school in an area that supports such activities. If opera provides you with the same outlet, check out the local offerings by looking in travel and tourism guides and by going on the Internet or to your campus library to read newspapers from areas you are considering. While you may, in fact, be too busy to really enjoy many outside activities, it may make you feel better to know that they are there, and if you stick around for breaks, you could take the opportunity to enjoy a concert or a long hike.

If you have a family you will be taking with you to medical school, you will want to consider additional aspects of location, including the job market, public and private schools, and the cost of child care (some universities offer subsidized day care to students—ask about this if it's a factor for you). You will want to consider medical school like any other relocation and select the place where you can get the education you need to pursue your career, balancing this with a location suitable to your entire family. Medical school will be stressful enough without concerns over your spouse's unemployment or the lack of affordable day care.

Additional Factors

Members of Minority Groups

You may have factors particular to your circumstances that you must consider when deciding where you will apply to medical school. Minority students may want to look for a school with a diverse student body, minority recruitment programs, and minority enrichment programs, all of which are available at some U.S. medical schools. Such programs provide a support network intended not only to recruit greater numbers of minority students into the field of medicine, but also to help them succeed in medical school. Some minority enrichment programs are for high school or precollege students and are designed to make students more competitive candidates for medical school. The AAMC publishes a guide to these programs, *Minority Student Opportunities in United States Medical*

Schools. Members of minority groups made up 11.6 percent of the new entrants to medical school in 1998–99, which is 110 more minority students than the previous year (MSAR 1999).

Students who are members of minority groups should also check with the minority affairs offices of the medical schools in which they are interested; if the school has no minority affairs office, inquire about minority programs at the student affairs or admission offices. As mentioned in Chapter 2, the AAMC offers the Medical Minority Applicant Registry (Med-MAR) to minority students who are applying to medical school. Any applicant officially in a minority group that is underrepresented in medicine can have their biographical information and MCAT scores sent to minority affairs and admission offices of all U.S. medical schools free of charge. Students can opt to participate in this program when they take their MCAT (for more on the MCAT, see Chapter 2).

Women

Women applying to medical school may want to look for a medical school with an environment supportive to women. Women still face issues of harassment and discrimination, and many may find themselves questioning the practicality of medical school and how it will affect their relationships, particularly if they are parents. Some women students may need maternity leave while in medical school, and child care, while it affects both parents, is often more of a burden to mothers. Overall, though they made up less than half of the 1998–99 entering class (44.3 percent), women had better rates of acceptance than men: 43.2 percent of the women applicants were accepted, as compared to 41.7 percent of men applicants.

The number of women accepted to medical schools has increased slightly for each of the past five years, though the number of women applicants has been dropping since the peak of 20,031 applicants in 1996–97 (MSAR 1999). These acceptance rates are good news for women applicants, who still may find a medical establishment that is dominated by men at many schools. The figures above are overall figures, of course, and not all schools will have rates of acceptance favorable to women. Women applicants should check with medical schools on the number of female applicants accepted and the residency programs into which women are matched, as well as the number of women faculty members. Some areas of specialization remain dominated by women, and others seem the exclusive domain of men. If you are a woman interested in pediatrics, this information may not impact you, but if you want to go into one of the surgical fields, you would be wise to look for a mentor within your medical school program who might help prepare you to compete for difficult-to-obtain residencies.

Women faculty members in U.S. medical schools currently comprise 26 percent of the total faculty (MSAR 1999). The AAMC Women in Medicine Program creates programs that are aimed at increasing the number of women faculty members in U.S. medical schools and at increasing the number of female faculty members in leadership positions. All U.S. medical schools have representatives from this program, which is called Women Liaison Officers (WLO). Chapters of the American Medical Women's Association (AMWA), which can be found on many campuses, are good resources for information on women practicing medicine, and women applicants can often find housing for interview visits through this organization. Certain private funding sources are also reserved for women students, and the AMWA has a loan program for women. For more information, contact the AMWA at their Web site (http://www.amwa-doc.org).

International Students

International students may have special needs when applying to U.S. medical schools. In 1998–99, only 146 international students entered medical school. This is less than 1 percent of the entering class. The low number of international medical students entering U.S. medical schools is in part because most U.S. medical schools give admission preference to students from their states. Proficiency in English is necessary for international applicants, who should note that the majority of financial aid available for medical students is federally funded, and international students are not eligible for this funding. It is quite difficult for international applicants to study medicine in the U.S., and if accepted, international students must be prepared to cover the costs of their medical education without the standard loan assistance that most U.S. students rely upon.

Nontraditional Applicants

Nontraditional students, who tend to be older than most applicants and have usually been removed from the academic environment for some time, may find the application process quite daunting, and they may also be without the academic support network most college students have at their disposal. The majority of students accepted to medical schools in 1998–99 were ages 20–23, and the best rates of acceptance were for those applicants under the age of 20 (MSAR 1999). Acceptance rates dropped steadily for applicants from age 23 to 38 and over, as did the number of applicants. Acceptance rates range from 34.8 percent for applicants ages 24–27 to 20 percent for applicants age 38 and over. Once you are over 24, it seems, you are less likely to be accepted to medical school than those applicants 23 and under, but the rates of acceptance do not decline steeply; with good preparation, your chances are not bad.

Postbaccalaureate programs may be necessary for older students to make themselves more competitive medical school applicants and to prepare them for medical school. These programs provide students with the premed background they need for medical school (and for the MCAT), as well as with premed advising. Postbaccalaureate programs often have full-time and part-time plans to help students get ready for medical school while remaining employed. (More information on postbaccalaurate programs is provided in Chapter 4.) While few nontraditional students enter medical school each year, they may be some of the most interesting candidates out there, in part because of the life experiences they bring with them. Nontraditional applicants, because they are usually making a career change, have likely thought long and hard about why they want to become doctors. If this is the case for you, include information on your life experiences and motivation for applying to medical school in your application essay.

Applicants with Disabilities

Students with disabilities also have special concerns when applying to medical school, and all students, regardless of disability, must be able to meet certain standards of technical ability as determined by each medical school. Students with disabilities should contact prospective medical schools for admission policies, which legally must comply with the American with Disabilities Act (ADA). These students will want to be sure that their disability will be accommodated at their medical school and that the school and clinical environment will be accessible. Students with disabilities are not required to disclose their disability, although it may be evident from the student's personal essay, reference letters, or MCAT scores (if the student was accommodated when taking the test, this may be evident on his or her score report). If you are concerned about your disability affecting your admission chances, you can ask that your letter writers not disclose it, and you can certainly leave it out of your personal statement, giving you the knowledge that you will make it through at least the first portion of the admission process without discrimination. Speak to your premed adviser about your concerns. If your adviser or your references, not to mention the medical schools you contact, are unhelpful and you believe it is because of your disability, contact the ADA representative on your campus.

EARLY DECISION PROGRAMS

Many U.S. medical schools offer early decision programs (EDP), which allow you to apply to one school that you agree to attend if offered admission. Obviously, if your number-one school does not have an early decision program, you will not want to use this option. Even if it does, think carefully before deciding to apply to an EDP, because you will be prohibited from applying to other programs until you have been rejected by the EDP school (or until after October1, whichever comes first). You will hear from them early—by October 1 for American Medical College Application Service (AMCAS) schools—but if you are not accepted, you will then be far behind your peers with any additional applications you file, because AMCAS accepts all applications beginning June 1.

If you are a very strong candidate and you are absolutely sure you want to go to George Washington University, for example, EDP may be a good option. If you are accepted, you will know by October 1 where you will attend medical school without enduring the hassle of waiting for calls, the stress of interviews, and the cost of interview travel. If the school is an AMCAS school, your complete application will be due between June 1 and August 1, so you will not have to plan far ahead of your peers who are also applying through AMCAS. (For non–AMCAS schools, check the MSAR or contact the school directly regarding EDP policies and deadlines.) See Chapter 4 for a full description of the admission process, including AMCAS and non–AMCAS applications.

COMBINED PROGRAMS

Highly qualified high school seniors can apply to combined programs for the B.A./M.D. or B.S./M.D. at a number of U.S. medical schools. (This option is discussed in Chapter 2.) The MSAR includes a list of these programs, which are very competitive. If you are sure in high school that medicine is the career choice you want to make, you should research this option and discuss it with your family and your guidance counselor. You can apply to other undergraduate programs as well so that you will have other options if you are not accepted into the combined program. Combined programs have their benefits:

you may spend less time getting your M.D. than if you went the traditional route; while some programs take eight years, a number take only six or seven. Provided that you do well as an undergraduate, you are then guaranteed a slot in the medical school at your undergraduate institution, thus eliminating the entire painful application process described in this book.

You must be sure that medicine is the path for you and that you want to pursue medicine at the institution that offers the combined program. You should still do all the medical school research before applying and get the MSAR and catalogs from the undergraduate and medical schools that interest you to be sure that you will get the education you want and have the clinical or research opportunities you will need to pursue your goals. You will simply have to complete this research in high school. This is a difficult decision to make in high school, but if you are highly motivated, this may be a good option for you.

VISITING SCHOOLS

What should you expect when visiting schools? How many should you plan to visit? You should really try to at least visit your state school, arranging for an overnight stay and a tour of the campus and its medical school facilities. This one visit will give you the opportunity to see firsthand what medical school looks like from the inside. (You will have additional opportunities to visit medical schools during the interview stage of the application process, which is discussed in Chapter 4.) If you are able to stay overnight with a medical student, so much the better—you can speak with them about their medical school and application experiences and try to find out what life is really like for students at the school. Ask about the courses and the curriculum, the faculty, and the resources for students. During your tour, you will want to see the campus and facilities, including computer and research labs, classrooms, libraries, and departmental offices. You should also ask to see the hospital(s) affiliated with the university, in order to observe students at work during their clinical training. You may find, during the tour, that the campus facilities are great but the hospital is small and low-technology or vice versa.

These are things that can help you decide whether or not you should apply to a school, but it is unlikely that you will be able to visit many schools before you apply, mainly for financial reasons. You will have to pay for travel to your interviews during the fall of your senior year in college, and, unless you are independently wealthy, you may not have the time and money to fly around the country looking at schools to which you may not even apply. Do try and visit one local school, however, so that you have a point of comparison when you go on your interviews and to give you practice dealing with medical school admission offices later.

MAKING A SHORT LIST

You may start out with a list of forty or more schools that really interest you, but by the spring of your junior year, you should have whittled this down to a more manageable number of schools. You will have done this, with the advice of your premed adviser, by considering the many elements of selection. Research the schools carefully; talk to students at the schools, alumni, and your peers who are also researching. You will find the schools that seem to offer you the best fit—those whose interests, goals, and requirements match your own.

There is no safe number of schools to which you should apply for guaranteed acceptance, but according to the MSAR, in 1998–99, applicants applied to an average of 11.74 schools. The MSAR states that those applicants using the AMCAS application who applied to twenty or more AMCAS schools had an acceptance rate of 44.3

percent at those schools—about 2 percent above the average acceptance rate for that year (MSAR 1999).

To How Many Schools Should You Apply?

This is really a matter of personal choice (and budget and time), but based on the MSAR figures noted above, a dozen is a good number to focus on. Remember that the more schools you apply to, the greater your application costs (see Chapter 4 for more information on primary and secondary application fees). When compiling your list of schools, start with twelve as a goal, and if you find that your top, well-rounded list of schools is eight or ten or fourteen or eighteen, that's fine. Try hard to match yourself up with schools, and be sure to select a range. If there's a medical school whose standards you do not quite meet, do not sell yourself short; your excellent essay, outstanding recommendations, and volunteer experience with a local hospital may balance out your GPA and MCAT scores. Don't apply to many schools that seem outside your reach, and be sure to apply to a few for which you are extremely well qualified.

As mentioned above, it's a good idea to apply to your state school, because state schools generally accept more in-state than out-of-state students and because in-state tuition is much less expensive than out-of-state tuition. Because they have this financial consideration, state schools are usually quite competitive. Do not think that you can slide into your state university's medical school without effort; you will still need to be a great candidate if you hope to be accepted. Look into special programs offered in your region that may better your chances of acceptance: if you are an Arizona resident, you can apply to the University of Arizona College of Medicine, where you would pay $8,436 in tuition and fees for the 1998–99 academic year. In 1998–99, Arizona had no new out-of-state entrants among the 100 students accepted there. Arizona does, however, participate in the Western Interstate Commission for Higher Education (WICHE) program, so students from the participating states of Alaska, Montana, and Wyoming are also eligible to apply to the University of Arizona as in-state students. If you live in a western state and would like more information on WICHE, contact the program in Boulder, Colorado (telephone: 303-541-0282). A similar program is available at the University of Washington for residents of Washington, Wyoming, Alaska, Montana, and Idaho (WWAMI). For more information on this program, contact the University of Washington (e-mail: askuwsome@u.washington.edu).

THE APPLICATION

Now that you have compiled your short list of a dozen or so schools, you are ready to begin the application process. Because this process is so lengthy, you should have started researching schools early—have your list of schools ready to go by late spring of your junior year. In the next chapter, we will consider the application process in detail.

The Application Process

Chapter 4

WHAT DO MEDICAL SCHOOLS WANT?

Most medical schools are looking for motivated, mature, well-rounded, and academically qualified students with a demonstrated interest in medicine whose interests and career plans mesh with the objectives and goals of the medical school. Initially, medical schools will consider you based on quantitative factors, including your GPA and MCAT scores. If you prove academically qualified, you will then need to prove yourself based on qualitative factors, such as your maturity, motivation, integrity, and personality. If you also meet these requirements, you will still need to show that your career goals and medical interests are a good fit with the programs and objectives of the medical school. All in all, this is no easy feat. Let's begin with the quantitative: your application.

TYPES OF APPLICATIONS

You can find out which form a school uses by checking the MSAR or contacting the school directly. For all application forms, follow the instruction booklet carefully; use black ink or a typewriter, as required for most medical school applications; and make a copy of your completed applications and any correspondence for your records. There are three basic types of medical school applications: AMCAS, non–AMCAS, and AACOMAS.

AMCAS

Most U.S. allopathic schools utilize the Association of American Medical Colleges (AAMC) application process, which is called the American Medical College Application Service (AMCAS). The primary application form is available from the AAMC and is collected by the AMCAS, which distributes the application to the schools to which you want to apply. Generally, if a medical school wishes to pursue your application, they will send out secondary application materials to you. The AMCAS process is reviewed in depth in this chapter, as this is the most common application process.

Non–AMCAS Allopathic Schools

Those allopathic schools that do not participate in the AAMC program will have their own application materials, which you must obtain from them directly. These applications are similar to the AMCAS application in content, although you generally do not have to do the lengthy course listings and grade conversions required by AMCAS; non–AMCAS schools will ask that official transcripts be sent to them directly. The non–AMCAS United States schools are the University of Missouri–Kansas City, Columbia University, New York University, the University of North Dakota School of Medicine and Health Sciences, Brown University (Brown has an eight-year B.A./M.D. program, leaving few spaces for first-year medical students), Baylor University, Texas Tech University, and the University of Texas system, which includes Texas A&M University, the University of Texas Southwestern Medical Center at Dallas, the University of Texas Medical Branch at Galveston, the University of Texas–Houston Health Science Center, and the University of Texas at San Antonio. Canadian medical schools also do not use the AMCAS system. Be sure to follow school instructions regarding application materials and deadlines; these will vary from AMCAS deadlines.

AACOMAS

The nineteen U.S. osteopathic schools use the American Association of Colleges of Osteopathic Medicine Application Service (AACO-MAS), which, like the AMCAS system, is a centralized service with one application form, which is sent to AACOMAS. (Portions of the AACOMAS application form are reprinted in Appendix B.) AACO-MAS then screens your application, and once your application is complete, processes the application using your official transcripts to verify the information you have given regarding course work. AACOMAS will not refund fees once processing has begun. An Applicant Profile is created from your application, and this profile, along with a copy of your full application, is forwarded to the schools you have designated on your application. A copy of the Applicant Profile will also be sent to you; you should read it carefully for any errors. Should you find an error, you must contact AACOMAS to update your profile.

Deadlines and Secondary Materials

AACOMAS applications are accepted beginning June 1, and processing takes six to eight weeks. Your application is not complete until your MCAT scores and official transcripts have been received by AACOMAS. If you plan to apply to an osteopathic school, designate AACOMAS as a recipient of your MCAT scores when you take the test (AACOMAS institution code: 600). If you decide after taking the MCAT to apply to an osteopathic school, you can request that an Additional Score Report be sent to AACOMAS. Contact the MCAT for additional reports (telephone: 319-337-1357). Transcripts must be sent to AACOMAS directly from all U.S. institutions you have attended, including universities and colleges, junior and community colleges, and trade and professional schools. Do not get copies of your transcripts and mail them with your application. To be considered official, transcripts must come from the registrar of each school you have attended. Be sure to list any Canadian or other international schools you have attended in your application. You should request that a set of all transcripts be sent to you as well as to AACOMAS; you will need them to complete your application.

Some osteopathic schools also offer early decision programs; keep this in mind when filing your applications, and file as early as possible if applying to early decision programs, giving yourself at least the six to eight weeks processing time required by AACOMAS before your deadline. Most osteopathic schools have rolling admission, which means that if you get everything in to AACOMAS in time for the University of Michigan College of Osteopathic Medicine deadline of December 1, for example, and they have been accepting applications since June 1, they will have been interviewing candidates for months prior to your submission, and your chances of obtaining a slot are not as good as they might have been had your application been in early.

Additional materials may be requested by individual schools, including a supplemental application form (complete with a supplemental application fee) and letters of recommendation. Generally, schools will request supplemental materials from you after reviewing your AACOMAS application. Students meeting certain minimum requirements are sent supplemental materials. Check the AACOM's Osteopathic Medical College Information Booklet, which, like the MSAR, lists information on each osteopathic school. Contact numbers, addresses, and Web sites are also given so that you can contact the schools directly for additional information.

Fees

The fee for the AACOMAS system is variable depending upon the number of schools to which you are applying. For one school, the fee is $50; for two, it is $95. You pay more for three, four, and so on, up to nineteen schools, the fee for which is $470. Should you decide to apply to additional schools after submitting your application forms, you can write to AACOMAS with your request: see the AACOMAS instruction booklet for details. AACOMAS offers a limited number of fee waivers, and if granted one of these, you may apply to three osteopathic schools without paying the standard AACOMAS fees. For your fourth and additional schools, you must pay the AACOMAS fees, beginning with the $50 fee for your fourth school. Instructions for the fee waiver can be found in the AACOMAS instruction booklet and entails forwarding AACOMAS a copy of your Student Aid Report (SAR), which you receive from the U.S. Department of Education after filing a Free Application for Federal Student Aid (FAFSA; see Chapter 5 for more on the FAFSA and student financial aid).

Another option for the fee-waiver application is to complete a College Scholarship Service (CSS) PROFILE; the resultant Needs Analysis Form should then be sent to AACOMAS (code: 7363). Contact your university's financial aid office for information on how to file these. The AACOMAS fee waiver does not include a waiver of secondary fees for individual schools, although if you receive a fee waiver from AACOMAS, they will forward this information to your designated osteopathic medical schools. You should also contact the schools directly for their fee-waiver policies.

AACOMAS application forms are available from AACOMAS directly (telephone: 301-968-4190) or electronically at the AACOM Web site (http://www.aacom.org). The AACOMAS by Computer (ABC) form is also available on diskette; call the AACOMAS number above to request a copy. If you have applied to an osteopathic medical school using AACOMAS before, you will need to start over with all new application materials, including MCAT scores and transcripts.

> "Be real. Don't try to fake it on the application, essays, or interviews."
> —medical student, Baylor College of Medicine

ELEMENTS OF AN APPLICATION

See Chapter 1 for a detailed time line of the application process.

The AMCAS Application Process

The AMCAS application process was developed by medical school admission officers in an effort to simplify the application process. AMCAS coordinates and distributes your application but does not make any admission decisions. Currently, 113 allopathic medical schools participate in the AMCAS application system, so if you are planning to apply to allopathic schools, chances are that you will be using this system. This is good for you, because if you are applying to twelve AMCAS schools, you will need to fill out only one primary AMCAS application. The AMCAS application is processed by AMCAS, which will forward your application to the schools you have specified.

Fees

The AMCAS fee schedule is similar to that of the AACOMAS; one schedule applies to initial school designations and a second schedule for additional designations. Each schedule is on a per-school basis, with the initial schedule of $55 for one school up to $525 for fifteen schools. The fee is then $30 for each school above fifteen on the initial form. For additional school designations, the fees range from $30 for one school to up to $500 for fifteen schools, with an additional $30 for each school over fifteen. The AMCAS fees are payable by check, U.S. money order, or credit card.

AMCAS offers a fee-waiver program that allows qualified students to apply to up to ten medical schools without paying the AMCAS fee. (Secondary fees are not affected by this waiver; more information on secondary fees is available later in this chapter.) Forms for the AMCAS Fee Waiver Program are included in your application packet. AMCAS begins accepting these applications on May 15 and will not accept them after December 1. You will be notified by mail that your request has been approved or denied, and if approved, you will receive a Fee Waiver Card to be submitted with your application. You must send this card with your application, and you cannot apply for a waiver once your application has been sent to AMCAS.

Other AMCAS Forms

The paper AMCAS application is available from participating medical schools, as well as from your premedical adviser and from the AAMC directly in April of each year (for the class entering in fall of the following year; in April 2000, the application for the class entering in fall 2001 is available). Check the AAMC Web site (http://www.aamc.org) for more information. The AMCAS application is also available in an electronic format (the AMCAS-E) at the AAMC Web site. Using software supplied at the site, you may complete your application and submit it to the AAMC on diskette, while also producing a copy for yourself. Portions of the AMCAS application form are reprinted in Appendix B.

Also available at the AAMC site are an electronic Fee Waiver Request Form, an Additional Designation Form (to add schools to your application list after your application has been submitted), and a Post Submission Change Form (to alter information already submitted). AMCAS will not accept applications until June 1 of each year, and application deadlines vary from school to school. Many schools have a rolling admission process (they will consider applications as they receive them, and those who have their applications in early will receive requests for secondary materials first) so you should get your AMCAS application in early. School deadlines are available in the MSAR, as well as from the schools directly. While it is best to get your application in early, do not send it before June 1, or it will be returned to you unprocessed.

Note that if you are applying for early decision programs, AMCAS must have your application by August 1 (transcripts are accepted within two weeks after this deadline). If you have applied to medical school using the AMCAS system in the past and are now reapplying, you must start again with a new application (including your MCAT scores and transcripts). If you are applying to a school as part of a special B.A./M.D. or B.S./M.D. program or as a student who deferred admission, you must file the Special Program/Delayed Matriculant Form, which can be obtained from your medical school.

The Application Packet

Your AMCAS application packet includes two copies of the AMCAS application. It is wise to use one as your practice application, which you can take to your premed adviser for assistance should you have questions. You should proofread your application carefully (and then proofread it again) before submitting it to AMCAS. Do not lose credit with medical schools for sloppy spelling or grammar errors or for errors with dates on your application. The packet also includes an instruction booklet with a sample application, both of which will help you in completing your application. The first page of the application requests biographical information, including the schools you have attended, your awards, your activities, and your employment history. Don't go crazy here: do not list awards you received in high school, and do not list dozens of extraneous activities. Rather, list honors and awards received in college (the most important first) and your most important activities. You should reiterate the items you mention later in your application, in your essay, in your letters of recommendation, and in your interview. Keep in mind that you want to present a coherent and consistent image of yourself to the admission committee. The second page is the Personal Comments or essay section—this is very important and is discussed in depth later in this chapter.

The Academic Record portion of the application (pages 3–4) is the final portion of the application, and can be frustrating: you must follow the AMCAS abbreviations for academic status, terms, courses, and type codes, and you will also have to list all courses you have taken, including transcript grade, and translate this grade to the corresponding AMCAS grade (AMCAS provides a Grading Systems

Conversion Table in the instruction booklet, and the electronic version of AMCAS makes this conversion for you). You will, of course, need copies of your transcripts from all schools you have attended to complete this section. Be certain of your answers: AMCAS will check the data you list in this section against the official transcripts they receive, and discrepancies will delay the processing of your application. If your transcripts or MCAT scores are not received by AMCAS, your application will not be processed. Be sure to have your MCAT scores sent to AMCAS by designating AMCAS as a score recipient on the day you take the test. If you need to have the scores sent to AMCAS later, you will need an Additional Score Report, which is available on the AAMC Web site (http://www.aamc.org).

Please follow all instructions in the instruction booklet. Do not try to be creative on your application; rather, follow the booklet exactly. Unanswered or incorrectly completed portions of the application will delay processing.

Once your application is verified, you will receive a Transmittal Notification and a copy of your application from AMCAS. You should check the information on your transmittal notice carefully and submit any corrections in writing to AMCAS. The AMCAS application packet includes a Biographic Change Form, an Academic Change Form, and an Additional Designation form for making such changes. AMCAS will send the revised information to you and to your designated schools; by the time you receive your Transmittal Notification, your application will have been sent to your designated schools. You should begin hearing from medical schools within two to three weeks of receiving your Transmittal Notification, and if you have not heard from any of your designated schools within three weeks, you may want to contact admission offices. Schools may ask you to complete secondary materials or request an interview at this point. Do not contact AMCAS regarding your status at particular schools, which make their decisions independent of AMCAS.

If you decide to withdraw your application, you must notify AMCAS in writing before the verification process is complete. If your application is withdrawn, your fees will be refunded, less a $55 service fee. After the application is withdrawn, it cannot be resubmitted for that application year.

Transcripts

As part of your AMCAS application, you are required to have one set of official transcripts sent to AMCAS for each school you have attended, including junior colleges, community colleges, trade schools, professional schools, universities or colleges, and graduate schools. To be official, these transcripts must be sent by the registrar directly to AMCAS. AMCAS accepts transcripts beginning March 15.

Using your transcripts, AMCAS will verify your academic record as listed on your application and will calculate your GPA and total credit hours. These numbers and a copy of your application are then forwarded to the medical schools to which you have chosen to apply.

Essay

The section of the AMCAS application titled Personal Comments (on page 2) is your opportunity to present a more personal side of yourself than the data on the rest of your application indicates. You should think carefully about what you want to say and the presentation you are trying to make with your entire application. The essay will likely be read many times as your application is being considered, and a really good essay can mean the difference between moving on to the interview or being left in the rejected applicants pile.

Do not try to condense your entire academic career or your life into the essay. Rather, it may be best to select a defining moment from your life or your college career that has brought you to where you are today. The application committee will be able to tell that you are well educated and involved from the rest of your application. They will not, however, know what a mature, caring individual you are unless you show them this side of yourself in your essay. Make your essay personal and try to tell an interesting story, but do not get overly emotional and do not embellish the details of your story. If you were moved toward a career in medicine when your Aunt Jessie was stricken with breast cancer, tell that story, but do not make up details (or invent such a story), or your essay will not ring true. Be honest about what has made you choose to apply to medical school, and if your only reason is truly that your father is a doctor, consider what kind of candidate that makes you. You may decide to discuss a research project you were involved in or your volunteer work at a community hospice; make sure the topic is important to you and that your sentiments are genuine. You may be asked about your essay in your interview, and a lack of sincerity on your part will come shining through in person.

Write and rewrite your essay. Be sure to practice your essay, drafting and editing it so that it is well written and error free. Read it aloud and have others read it as well. Your premed adviser may be helpful to you in preparing your essay, and if grammar or spelling are not your strong suit, have someone who is better equipped proofread your essay. Be prepared to work hard on this element of your application. It must fit into the space provided on page 2 of the application and cannot be smaller than 10-point type (see the sample application in Appendix B). Do not attach additional pages to the application (although you may print out your essay and paste it to the application form in the space provided), and do not expect to change your essay or send it at a later date. Many medical school admission committees place a great deal of weight on this section of your application, because it will show what a well-rounded person you are—you not only excel in your science courses, but also are personable and communicate well in writing. Sample application essays may be found in Appendix C.

Secondary Application Materials

After the medical schools receive your AMCAS application, they will notify you directly of any supplemental and/or secondary materials you must send to complete your application. These materials may include additional transcripts, additional fees, letters of recommendation, and an interview. Again, the school will contact you directly for this information, and materials should be sent to the individual school and not to AMCAS. Some schools send out secondary application materials to all applicants, and some evaluate the applications, culling the more promising candidates and sending secondary materials to those applicants only. If you are asked to complete secondary materials, take this as a promising sign and complete all materials and return them as soon as possible—certainly prior to the school's application deadline. Once the school has your complete application, they can process it and decide whether they will invite you for an interview. If you want a head start on the secondary materials, check with your premed adviser, who may have secondary application materials on file for many schools.

Secondary Fees

Most medical schools require that you pay an application fee directly to them; some only require this fee with secondary materials if you move on to that level. The fee ranges from $15 to $100 and must be received by the school's application deadline. A few medical schools, including the University of Arizona College of Medicine, the University of Florida College of Medicine, the Medical College of Georgia School of Medicine, the Uniformed Services University of the Health Sciences F. Edward Hébert School of Medicine, the University of Mississippi School of Medicine, and the University of Texas System, do not require a separate fee. For these schools, the AMCAS fee is the only fee you will have to pay in the application process.

Recommendations

Letters of recommendation will tell the schools to which you apply a lot about you and your interactions with others, and it is essential that you have resplendent recommendations in your application files. Keep this element in mind as you go through undergraduate school, and develop relationships with professors from whom you want recommendations. These professors should have the opportunity to get to know you and should not be important campus personalities with whom you have had little or no contact. Certainly, if there is a prominent professor at your university whose work interests you, you should try to take classes with him or her or, perhaps, work on a research project with the professor so that he or she will be qualified to write you a recommendation. You may want to attend student-faculty gatherings so that you have the opportunity to meet your professors under less formal circumstances. If you have a well-known professor whom you know but with whom you have a personal conflict or in whose classes you have done poorly, do not ask this professor to recommend you to a medical school admission committee. It will do you no good to have a lukewarm recommendation from a star professor, and if the professor does not believe in your qualifications or does not know you well, the recommendation will likely damage your application. On the other hand, it will also not benefit you to have amazing letters of recommendation from your Uncle Joe, who is a pediatrician, or from other family and friends. The people who write your recommendations should be qualified to evaluate you objectively as a candidate for medical school, and with that in mind, admission committees are often specific in their requirements for these letters.

Quite often, your premedical adviser (or premedical committee, if your university has one) will write one of your recommendations; this recommendation is required by some medical schools. Other good choices are professors with whom you have taken several courses (and done very well) or with whom you have worked. Be sure that the professors you are considering are aware of your plans to attend medical school, as this may change the way they interact with you. You do not want to surprise your physics professor with this information when you ask her to recommend you, but rather, have her consider you a potential medical student from the beginning. You may find a mentor along the way or may receive helpful advice from professors who followed the medical school path in their career.

It can be difficult to ask professors for recommendations, but having a relationship with the professors you ask will make the task easier. Remember that professors write such letters frequently, and your request will not likely be unusual. When requesting recommendations, ask your professors if they feel they can write a solid letter of recommendation for you. If they are less than confident, or offer any kind of excuse (how busy they are, that they are leaving for the Philippines in the morning), let them know that you will ask another professor and thank them for their consideration. It may be uncomfortable for you to know that this professor cannot recommend you, but it is best to find this out before they write an impersonal or less than splendid letter on your behalf. Be sure to give your letter writers plenty of time to write their letters; do not wait until the fall of your senior year to ask for recommendations, but instead ask in the spring of your junior year, and follow up with your professors (without making a nuisance of yourself). You should have the letters in hand by September of your senior year, when you will begin hearing from medical schools requesting secondary materials.

Help your letter writers as much as possible. Be specific with your professors about your plans and interests and offer them backup materials, such as your resume, transcript, and any relevant publications, to familiarize them with your abilities and interests of which they may not be aware. Always provide your letter writers with stamped, addressed envelopes in which to mail their confidential recommendations. Go over your list of professors with your premed adviser, who may know which faculty member writes a great letter and which one always misses the deadline. Most medical schools will give you the option of sending confidential letters of recommendation or those that you have read. It is generally best to offer your letter writers confidentiality, as this may encourage them to speak more freely about you (whether good or bad). If you are not comfortable giving your professors this leeway, you may want to reconsider whom you have asked to write your recommendations. If these are professors who know you and believe in your abilities, you have nothing to lose by having them send a confidential letter of recommendation to your medical school, and if you do not send confidential letters, your medical schools may wonder why.

Interview

Once you have made it to the secondary application level and have returned all of your secondary materials to your preferred schools, you must wait for the next stage, the interview. If you were applying to other graduate programs—in history or geography, for example— you would not be required to visit the school and be interviewed by faculty members. You would be accepted based on your application information. However, medical school applicants must be interviewed before they are accepted. This means that the interview is very important to your application, which is worrisome for many students. You should, however, look at the interview as your opportunity to distinguish yourself from the hundreds of other applicants the admission committee has seen on paper.

If you do not hear from schools regarding interviews within a few weeks after your AMCAS application, you should contact their admission departments, but remember that schools interview fairly continuously through the fall, winter, and spring. If you are not asked for an interview in the fall, you may still be asked as part of a later round of candidates. If you are asked for an interview, you have made it over the first hurdle: the school finds your academic record and MCAT scores acceptable. Almost uniformly, medical schools do not offer admission to candidates until after the interview, and most medical schools will only interview those candidates they are seriously considering; if you make it to this stage with a few of your choices, you are more likely to be accepted—provided that you do well at the interview.

It is difficult to tell you what to expect of the interview process; partly because it is an unknown element; it is the most nerve-wracking part of the application process for many potential medical students. Obvious pointers are to be punctual and dress well. If

> "[I]n general, they really just want to get to know who you are.
> They're not trying to trick you or embarrass you, they're just trying to
> get to know the real you. So your best bet is to be yourself. I also
> recommend reviewing your personal statement before the interview,
> because they take a lot of questions from that."
>
> —Dr. Sachin Shah, former medical student, Villanova–MCP
> Hahnemann University accelerated program

you're nervous already, don't overdo the caffeine on the morning of
your interview. Wear a suit of a conservative hue (complete with a
tie) if you are a man; women should also dress conservatively, in a
skirt or pantsuit, and all candidates should wear a minimum amount
of jewelry and makeup (and sensible shoes, in case a tour is part of
your interview experience). While the interview is the place to let
your personality win over the admission committee, flashy clothing,
makeup, or jewelry may get the attention of the interviewer but may
also deflect attention from what you have to say and who you are: you
want them to remember you, not your many piercings. The interview is your opportunity to let the admission committees know that
you are a mature, self-possessed person with integrity and a genuine
interest in helping others. Some of these qualities may have been
evident from your application materials, but the impression you
make in the interview will go a long way toward deciding whether or
not a school finds you an acceptable candidate for their program.

When you enter the interviews, address your interviewers by
name and firmly shake hands with them. Then be prepared to dive
right in. This is where all your hard thought on why you want to
become a medical doctor may be useful. You will likely be asked a few
questions related to your application and interests. On the other
hand, your interviewer may spend much of the interview asking you
questions unrelated to your medical interests to get a better idea of
who you are. You may be asked about your personal experiences and

goals or to elaborate on your impressive application essay. You may be asked to respond to "what if" situations about a current issue in the news (try to keep up on current events) or about ethical issues facing medical doctors today.

Things you should not be asked include your marital status, if you are planning to have children, how old you are, or your sexual orientation. You may still be asked these questions, which AMCAS and most school policies prohibit. If you are asked an inappropriate question, what should you do? You may feel justifiably angry, but you should not let this register: do not lose your composure in the interview. You may want to politely answer around the question or refuse to answer the question at all. You also have the option of answering the question (truthfully or not), and you can register a complaint with the department following the interview (or in the postinterview questionnaire some schools provide). Honestly, your best bet may be to answer the question and move on to your next interview. If you offend the interviewer or the department, your chances of admission may be damaged; on the other hand, it may be more important to you to maintain your integrity than to attend a school that allows such interview practices.

Your interview will likely last between 30 minutes and 1 hour, and you may be interviewed by a single representative of the admission committee, by the entire committee, or by several members of the committee. Be prepared for a one-on-one situation, but do not be surprised to find yourself faced with a group of people who may all ask you questions, or even in an interview with several other applicants—this is not the norm, but it can happen. Your interviewer may be completely familiar with your application, they may have been given your personal statement to read, or they may not have had access to your application file at all (some schools do this to keep the interviewer objective). After the interview, thank your interviewer and shake his or her hand again.

> "Make a coherent career plan that plays on your strengths and present it during your interview. You won't be forced to follow it later, and it sounds a lot more impressive than 'I dunno.'"—former medical student, University of Texas Southwestern Medical Center at Dallas

You should prepare for the interview as much as possible. Some students go so far as to videotape themselves in their interview outfits being interviewed by a fellow student or premed adviser. This may seem like overkill, but it can be a very useful tool—you may be surprised to find that you speak very quickly or often insert "like" or "um" into your sentences, that you do not make eye contact, that you have a nervous foot-tapping or hair-touching habit, or that your outfit makes you look ill or your lipstick is too bright. With enough time and practice, you can learn to speak more slowly, train yourself out of the distracting or annoying habits you have, or decide to modify your interview outfit. You want to present yourself as poised and confident, and again, you want the interviewer to be impressed with you and not your outfit or your key-jiggling.

Before each interview, you should prepare specifically for that school. Remind yourself why you chose to apply there—you may be asked this. Reconsider the school's mission statement, selection factors, and areas of special interest, and be prepared to present yourself as the best possible candidate for that school. Review your application materials—both your AMCAS application and the school's secondary application. Check with your premed adviser to see if any graduates of your college are attending the university with which you will be interviewing, and if so, see if your adviser can put you in touch with them. A current student's input can be invaluable to you before your interview. If you've made it to the interview, you're one step closer to acceptance, but you're also in much stiffer competition. The group of students with whom you are competing are the most qualified students the school could find, and regardless of how stellar your GPA and MCAT scores may be or how heart-breaking your essay is, the interview is your one chance to distinguish yourself to the interviewers and to make a solid impression on them as a great candidate for their program. Most schools interview many more applicants than they will ultimately accept—some interview as many as ten times the number of spaces they will have open. The interview is an essential stage of the application process, and you cannot blow it, or you will all but surely miss your chance at acceptance.

Because you will have to foot the bill for your interviews, you may want to try to group them together, planning your northeast interviews during one 3-day period and your west coast interviews during a later week. If you haven't heard from one of your west coast schools, call the department and let them know that you are planning a trip west for interviews. Schools will usually let you know if they plan to interview you. Many schools will have housing suggestions for your stay, and some will provide you with overnight accommodations with another medical student on campus. Bring your luggage as carry-on; scrounging for clothes the morning of the interview because of lost luggage is not a situation in which you want to find yourself. Plan your trip as far in advance as possible for the best rates from airlines, car rental agencies, and hotels. Look into possible discounts from airlines, and also check with discount agents. There are many sites on the Web that offer airfare discounts. There is no easy way around it: the interview process may be very expensive, and you should plan ahead the summer before your senior year by trying to save extra money in preparation for your travels.

Here is a bit of final advice on interviews. Do not become overwrought at the thought of the interview process, which all medical school candidates must endure. The interview is your opportunity to consider each medical school, the faculty, and the program, gathering information that will help you decide which school to attend when you receive your acceptances. If you have not had the opportunity to visit the campus prior to your interview, arrange for a tour later on your interview day (this is often a planned part of your day, but ask to be sure). Check out the department offices, the libraries, and graduate housing. You may even want to see one of the medical facilities associated with the medical school. Medical students may conduct your tour. Ask them questions and try to make a good impression; they may be asked for feedback from the committee. Be pleasant with everyone you meet, from med students and professors to department administrative staff members. You want to make a good impression all around.

Ask beforehand if the department arranges accommodations with medical students on campus, as this would be a good opportunity for you to get a medical student's perspective on the program. The medical school is not only interviewing you, but you are interviewing it. If you have questions about the program, do not hesitate to ask, and remember that you may be asked for your questions: it's better to have prepared an intelligent and pertinent question than to have none at all. If you feel your interview did not go well, don't dwell on this, but try and learn from the experience so that the interview you have at your next school will go much better. There will be times when you just don't click with your interviewer or when he or she seems not really interested or familiar with you as a candidate. Continue to do your best in such situations.

Here are some sample interview questions:

- Why do you want to study medicine?
- Why are you the best candidate for our medical program?
- What are your goals for the next 10 years?
- What are your thoughts on physician-assisted suicide?
- What do you think of health maintenance organizations?

HOW TO KEEP IT ALL ORGANIZED

From the moment you begin considering medical schools, you should begin a system to organize your medical school information. In the beginning, you may only need one file or folder, but later, as you research individual schools, you should work out a system to keep all materials for each school together: catalogs, applications, and notes from your tour or from your talk with a student there. Keep a checklist within each file for schools to which you decide to apply, and check off the requirements as you meet them. You will also need separate files for your MCAT notes and study guides, your AMCAS and/or AACOMAS applications, and financial aid and scholarship materials. You will need to keep important dates and times marked on a calendar or datebook (a datebook is generally better, as it is more portable than a wall calendar) to remind you of the MCAT registration and test dates, study dates, meetings with your premed adviser, meetings with professors who will write your recommendations, application deadlines, and interview dates and times. You may want to create a monthly tickler or reminder file that will remind you when it is time to follow up regarding recommendations, what materials are due that month, and when you should call schools to check on your application status. Do not underestimate your need to be organized during the medical school application process. If you are late for appointments, misplace important information, or miss deadlines, it will not only reflect poorly on you, but may adversely affect your chances of getting into medical school.

HOW TO DECIDE WHICH SCHOOL TO ATTEND

You've Been Accepted!

One of the most important decisions you will make in your medical career is where to attend medical school. This is the time to go back to the choices you made earlier about where to apply and why. You likely have ranked the schools to which you applied and know which is your top choice, but you'll want to reconsider the schools to which you have been accepted now that you have visited the campus and met with faculty members in your interview. You may decide that the atmosphere at the school you ranked seventh actually suits you much better than the third-ranked school to which you were also accepted. You will also want to consider the financial aid packages each school offers you. For more on financial aid and selecting a medical school, see Chapter 5.

Important factors noted by students in deciding which medical school to attend include clinical emphasis, cost, facilities, financial assistance, location (urban or rural, close or not close to home), prestige, program flexibility, quality of life, reputation, and research strength.

Each medical school will have its own earliest and latest dates for offering acceptance; for most schools, the earliest date is October 15, and positions will be offered until the class is full. (Early Decision Program applicants will usually be notified earlier.) Generally, you will have a minimum of two weeks from the date of an offer to make your decision to accept or reject the offer, although some schools are more generous with this time frame. These deadlines are available in the MSAR and from the schools. If you were anxious to have a place, you may have accepted the first offer of admission you received, and later, you may have been accepted to a school you would prefer to attend. This is not an unusual situation and is one for which AMCAS and the medical schools are prepared. As an applicant, you are obligated to hold no more than one acceptance at a given time. If you receive several offers at once, you should accept your first choice, and decline the other offer(s) in a timely manner, so that those slots can be offered to other candidates. If you have accepted a position and are then offered admission by a school you would prefer, you should withdraw your original acceptance and accept the new offer.

Deferred Entry

Perhaps you have been accepted to a school you would like to attend, but for personal reasons, you feel you cannot enter for the year in which you have applied. In such a case, you may wish to defer your entry to the school. Deferral policies vary from school to school, although some permit deferred entrance for one or more years. The MSAR gives general information on deferral, but if you may need to defer, you should check with your schools regarding their policies. You should request a deferral from your medical school no later than when you respond to their offer of admission.

WHAT TO DO IF YOU DON'T GET IN (THIS TIME)

Do you know why you were not accepted? If not, you should sit down with all of your application materials and consider your qualifications and the requirements of the schools to which you applied. Call a few of the schools to which you applied and speak with someone in admission. If you were interviewed at several schools, contact them first. If you were not asked to interview, call several of the schools you thought were most likely to admit you. Let the admission representative know that you would like to make yourself a better candidate before reapplying, and ask what might make you a better candidate for their program. You may want to arrange a phone appointment with a counselor after explaining your needs to give them the opportunity to review your application file again. Encourage the person you speak with to be candid about your future chances for acceptance—you want them to be as forthright as possible. You will not be helped by general comments such as, "We had a very strong group of applicants this year." Specific information, such as that your GPA or MCAT scores were too low, that your interview was not stellar, or that the school is simply looking for applicants with specific interests, will be most helpful to you in reapplying, should you decide to do so.

Postbaccalaureate Programs and Other Options

Once you have spoken with an admission officer, you should consider your options and discuss the situation with your premedical adviser. You may decide that medical school is not for you after all, and you will want to pursue other career possibilities in health or other fields. If your MCAT scores were the problem, perhaps you will want to take an MCAT preparation course before retaking the test. If the problem was your grades, you may need to retake your science courses, which could mean applying to postbaccalaureate programs. Postbaccalaureate programs are generally one- to two-year science programs that are meant to prepare students to apply to medical schools. Some postbaccalaureate programs are geared toward nontraditional students and those who received their bachelor's degrees in nonscience subjects and must complete premed courses and get premed counseling. Others intend to increase the number of minority students accepted to medical school. There are full-time and part-time programs. Some are much more structured than others, and some are affiliated with particular medical schools. You should select a postbaccalaureate program carefully: this is an expensive option. Your premed adviser should be able to recommend such a program to you—there are more than 100 available in the U.S., and they vary in quality and size. The AAMC Web site also includes a list of postbaccalaureate programs. Some of them are quite reputable and have medical school acceptance rates near 90 percent for their graduates. If you enter a postbaccalaureate program, be prepared to work hard: you must do well in all of your classes. When you finish your postbaccalaureate program, you will have a graduate degree in the sciences. Many medical schools do not consider graduate grades, however, and your postbaccalaureate experience may not help your chances of admission significantly.

If you lacked enough experience or your interview was your weak point, you should perhaps spend a year volunteering or interning with a physician or hospital or working with the public in some capacity—perhaps train as an emergency medical technician. Other medical school options include osteopathy, for those who have applied only to allopathic schools; graduate programs in the sciences; and international medical schools. If you decide to apply to osteopathic schools, research osteopathic medicine and consider different osteopathic schools as you did when selecting your allopathic medical schools. Be certain that osteopathic medicine will offer you the training and career you want as a medical doctor and that the osteopathic philosophy is one with which you agree before you apply. Graduate programs in the sciences are another option that could better your chances of getting into medical school; this is a costly and time-consuming option, however, so make sure you genuinely want to pursue the subject of your degree. Your chances of getting into medical school will not necessarily increase, because as mentioned above, some medical schools do not consider graduate courses. It may also be difficult to get into graduate programs in the sciences. International medical school should probably be your last option, not only because of the language barrier you may face when studying abroad, but also because there is no guarantee that you can practice medicine in the U.S. once you obtain your degree. You will still have to pass licensing exams and acquire a residency, which is a very competitive process for students with U.S. medical degrees. An international degree could make things harder on you in the long run.

Before you decide to reapply to medical school, or to attend a postbaccalaureate program, you should think carefully about your reasons for becoming a doctor. This is not to say that you should not reapply, but you should remember how arduous the application process is and be prepared to start over again, resending transcripts and MCAT scores, getting new recommendations, awaiting responses from schools, and enduring the interviews again. If a medical career is truly what you want, don't give up. Make a game plan for the next application cycle, and stick with it until you are accepted.

Paying for Medical School

COSTS ASSOCIATED WITH MEDICAL SCHOOL

Debt, Debt, Debt

As you will know if you have begun researching medical schools, a medical education can be quite expensive these days. Debt is a natural and, many times, unavoidable part of medical school for most students. It is not unusual for medical students to graduate with $50,000 to $150,000 in student loan debt. This may seem outrageous to you, maybe even crazy or frightening, but you will find that within the medical school environment, such debt is commonplace. Not until you're in your residency, when you must begin paying back your loans (on an annual salary of $30,000 to $35,000), will the reality of your debt situation begin to sink in with those first few monthly payments that equal or exceed your rent.

Make a Budget!

You may think that budgeting is really a very simple matter for which you have little use, or perhaps you have never thought of budgeting and you have no idea where to begin. Either way, budgeting should be a big part of your financial future, and careful budgeting can help you get through medical school without constant worry over your finances. Budgets are important to financial aid offices, and you will find that each school to which you apply has a school budget for students, which is prepared by the school's financial aid office and printed in the university catalog. The university budget includes estimated costs for your tuition, school fees, and cost of living. The total of all aid you receive cannot exceed the university's budgeted amount. They will base your financial aid needs on this budget, and you should use their figures when making your own personal budget whether you plan to apply for financial aid or not.

Why Budget?

Why do you need a budget? To make the loan or grant money you receive carry you through each semester. You will have enough on your mind without worrying about how to pay next month's rent. What is a budget? It is simply a method of planning your finances in which you allocate your known income for your expenses. The goal is to have enough income to cover all of your expenses (and then some), which is why it is a good idea to have an estimated budget for yourself before you accept your medical school's financial aid package. You don't want to realize in mid-October that you really need another $2,000 per semester, and if you figure this out early enough, you can apply for additional aid or personal loans to keep your cash flow even. You also shouldn't accept loans in excess of what you will really need; do not plan to use the extra $5,000 for a nicer apartment or a down payment on a new car, because you will have to repay this later. If you have worked out a budget and have an idea of your expenses, you will also know where you can cut back to stay within your budget: you will know that you can get by with fewer trips to the salon or that you can plan to fly home for winter break but not spring break. Because you will presumably have a limited amount of money on which live while you are in graduate school, you will need to make careful decisions on how to spend your money. It will be difficult to do much planning before you know how much you will have to spend, but you can get started early by estimating your expenses. Start with simple categories.

Fixed and Flexible Expenses

Some of your expenses will be fixed. These are those costs you cannot control, including tuition and fees at your chosen medical school, your monthly rent (you control this amount until you actually select a place to live, of course, after which the amount is fixed), debt payments (including car loans, personal loans, and credit cards), taxes, insurance (auto, health, and home), and child care. Most of your other expenses will be flexible, meaning that you control the amount you spend on these categories. Flexible expenses include groceries, clothes, transportation, entertainment, travel, household expenses, books, and, to a certain extent, utilities (including telephone, gas, and electricity). This last category is not completely within your control; you will need electricity, but it is up to you whether you are conscientious about turning off lights and the TV and stereo, and you decide how many long distance phone calls you make. List all of the expense categories you can think of, and then try and estimate what you spend on them on a monthly basis. Hints on this are found in the following sections.

Tuition

The main cost of medical school is the fixed expense of medical school tuition. This cost is considerable at many institutions and should be a factor when you make your choice about which school to attend. You can spend $50,000 or $5,000 per year on tuition. Tuition is above and beyond all of the other costs you will have as a medical student. If you lived off campus as an undergraduate and you or your parents shelled out $10,000 or so to house you and keep you in snacks, CDs, and other essentials, consider how much more you will need as a medical student if your tuition is much greater and financial assistance is not forthcoming.

The cost of a school should not be the only point determining your choice, but if you are accepted to two schools, one of which has annual tuition of $12,000 and the other with annual tuition of $22,000, you will want to consider carefully whether the advantages of attending the more expensive school (if there are any) outweigh the burden of cost you will have to bear. How important is the name recognition of your school, the technology available there, the school's reputation in family (or other) medicine, or whatever else you have decided is important to you in selecting a medical school? If the less-expensive school is clearly the inferior choice, you may want to opt for the more expensive program and plan on getting larger loans to cover the cost of your education. In the long run, an M.D. is an M.D., and it may sound impressive that you went to Columbia, but at $28,008 per year, Columbia had better do more for you than impress your friends and relatives.

Look into the different rates for in-state and out-of-state tuition at most state schools. At the University of North Carolina at Chapel Hill School of Medicine, resident tuition is $2,502 per year. At the same school, nonresidents pay $22,984 per year. This kind of difference may make it worth your while to consider your home state's school. You may even want to look into establishing residency in another state in order to qualify for resident tuition rates. Check into this latter option carefully before you make your move, because residency requirements vary from state to state. You may need to move to the state and show proof of residency (driver's license and paid taxes) for one year prior to entering medical school, but check with the medical school, because universities usually have carefully drawn residency requirements of their own.

Of course, moving to another state for good rates does not guarantee you admission to the state school, but it may increase your admission chances; at the University of North Carolina at Chapel Hill, 140 of the 160 new students entering in 1998 were in-state students. Look before you leap; before you move to another state to save on tuition rates, know the state's residency requirements and whether your chances of admission will increase.

Living

Costs of living include food, transportation, clothing, medical costs, child care, entertainment, travel, and other household expenses. This last category can include everything from laundry and cleaning supplies to cable TV and subscriptions to haircuts and even postage stamps and pet care. When calculating your food costs, remember to include the daily coffee you buy, as well as restaurant meals and vending machine snacks. Transportation should include all of your auto expenses: car payments, insurance payments, gas, oil, auto repairs, and parking. This category should also include optional forms of transportation if these apply: subway or bus fare or bicycle maintenance. Medical costs can include your insurance and prescriptions, dental care, eye care, and even that therapeutic massage you need twice a month. Entertainment will have to cover movies and videos, records and books, and perhaps your subscriptions, and cable will go here as well. Travel may include your trips back east to visit family, as well as a summer vacation or transportation to a conference or summer internship.

Are you a single student, or do you have a spouse or partner and/or family? Having a partner can offset your costs if this person works and will help support you through medical school, but a family also means an increased cost of living for everything from food to laundry to health care. If you have children, a great expense will likely be child care. Be sure to check with your medical school to see if day-care services are available. Some schools provide day care for free or at reduced costs to students. Such programs can be life savers for strapped young families or single-parent medical students.

Books and Supplies

If you took science courses as an undergraduate—you likely have, if you're applying to medical school—you know how incredibly expensive science and math textbooks are. Get ready to continue spending piles of money on these texts, and don't forget about laboratory and other required supplies. If you need an idea of how much this part of your budget will cost, check the catalogs of a few medical schools; they usually list a general semester estimate. There is really no way around these costs; you can, of course, limit yourself to the least expensive notebooks, foregoing the Palm Pilot day planner and other high-technology accessories, but you will need the books required for your classes.

Do not plan on getting required texts from the library—either forty other students thought of this as well and got there before you, or the professor has the library copy on reserve. If the volume is on reserve, you may think you can get by using it a few hours daily in the reserve reading room, but you may find that you need the text in class, that many other students are using the book this way and it's difficult to get time with it, or that you do your best reading (or only have the time for it) at 3 a.m. in the comfort of your own kitchen. These reasons make it inconvenient for you to not have your own copy of the texts. (They may also be useful when you study for your USMLE boards.) You can save money by purchasing used textbooks, if these are available at your campus bookstore. Do not, however, purchase last year's books from your roommate, who is a year or two ahead of you—the texts may have changed, or revised editions may now be required. Be sure to check your reading list before buying text books outside the approved bookstores.

Reducing Living Costs

What can you do to keep your cost of living down? Shop around for inexpensive groceries, try not to eat out, check into economical health-care and child-care programs (many schools offer both of these to students), and car pool or live within walking or biking distance of your medical school campus. You may find that you simply have to cut back on some of the luxuries you previously enjoyed; you won't be around to watch that cable TV and won't have time for books and magazines anyway, and you may have to forego your daily coffee and paper, or at least that bimonthly massage. You will have to figure out for yourself which expenses are necessary and which are more frivolous—perhaps you really must have the Cartoon Network, but you find you can get along fine with a bicycle rather than a car. If a particular magazine or daily coffee is part of the routine that keeps you going, you can work this into your budget by cutting back in another area—not eating out, for example, or not buying clothes or music.

Housing/Utilities

Is subsidized housing available to graduate students on your campus? Most schools offer some kind of graduate student housing, which tends to be away from campus. At many universities, you will find that this housing may be far from campus, there may be few spaces available (some will be reserved for married graduate students), and the housing itself may be grim. When considering housing, you should compare the cost of graduate housing to off-campus housing. Most university towns have a wealth of off-campus housing for students, and you can often find shares by checking the school newspaper or the bulletin board or Web site of the university's housing department or the medical school. To start your budget before you actually rent a place, go to the Web or to your campus library and check the classified sections of local and campus newspapers in the city where your medical school is located. Scanning these ads for a few weeks will give you an idea of what shares, rented rooms, studios, apartments, and houses cost; you can speak with someone at the medical school to find out which neighborhoods are safe and close to campus. Use the ads to create a price range to plug into your budget. Once you've worked out your budget, you may find that houses are out your reach, but a one- or two-bedroom apartment is affordable. This will help you when it comes time for you to head to school and rent your apartment: you'll know what's in your price range before you look.

When looking for housing, you will want to consider not only cost, but also proximity to campus—is the apartment closer to campus the same cost as the one 15 miles north? If so, you may be able to save money by walking or biking to school if you live closer to campus, and you also may make it home for meals more often rather than spending all day on campus, dining there or nearby. Also consider whether any utilities are included with your rent, if there are laundry facilities available, and what type of heat or air-conditioning is provided (if you live in Tucson, it may be worth a little extra each month to get the apartment with central air). Do not rent more space than you need; just because a three-bedroom house in Lexington, Kentucky, is less expensive than your old studio in Brooklyn, New York, don't rent the larger space unless you need it for your family or have roommates to share your expenses. On the same note, don't try to live in a rented room if it's just not large enough, and don't rent in the worst part of town so that you'll have money left over for new CDs each month. Cost is important, but so is your comfort and safety.

Your utilities will include your phone, gas, electric, water, sewage, and garbage. Some rentals include the costs of heat and hot water or gas and electric. Do not assume that any costs are included in your rent, however, and if it's not spelled out, be sure to clarify this with the landlord. Renters are not often responsible for costs of sewage and garbage, but you will be responsible for your own phone service and for any other utilities not covered by your landlord. Some utilities will require a deposit; call local service providers to check on this, and consider it an up-front cost if you are responsible for this utility. (Often companies will spread this deposit billing out over several months, and it is usually a refundable amount required for new accounts. The deposit will be returned to you when you close your account or will be applied to unpaid amounts should you become delinquent in your payments.)

Reducing Housing Costs

How do you cut costs on housing and utilities? Shop around for the best rates on your phone and other utility services. Deregulation of phone and other services means greater competition for your business, and in many parts of the country, you may choose not only your long-distance and local phone service carriers but also your gas or electricity supplier, so compare rates before signing up for a utility provider. Select your housing carefully, and consider living with friends or family members if any are nearby. Also consider finding a roommate or becoming one to save money on rent and utilities, and live close to campus if this will save on transportation or other costs.

Cost-Cutting Strategies for Medical Students

Once you've made a preliminary budget, you may find that you will need to cut costs in order to keep to your budget. How can you do this? Below is a list of a few cost-cutting tips.

- Live at home or with a roommate.
- Shop around for the best prices on your telephone and other utilities.
- Buy used textbooks.
- Try to eat at home or take food with you whenever possible (this is both more economical and healthier than eating most meals out).
- Stay away from credit cards whenever possible.

This last tip is very important to your credit future. Do not use a credit card to pay for things your budget simply will not afford (new clothes, CDs, gifts, or travel), and especially do not use a credit card (or credit card convenience checks) to pay for tuition, rent, or other bills. This is a terribly expensive way to supplement your income. Whereas most subsidized student loans have interest rates of 8 percent or less, credit cards generally have interest rates of 10 to 25 percent. If you rack up thousands of dollars of debt on your credit card, you may find yourself unable to make the minimum payments, which will likely only cover your interest each month; you probably did not include credit card payments in your budget.

Remember that credit card debt is not deferrable; while you are not required to make any payments on your student loans until you leave school (or attend school less than half-time), your credit card payments are due each month, as soon as you use the card. If you fail to make your payments or do not make them on time, this can affect your credit rating down the road, when you are trying to get a loan for a car or home. You may want to use your credit card for purchases because of a special deal—perhaps airline miles—but do not buy anything on credit that you do not have the budgeted money to pay for, and if you do use your credit card for everyday purchases, *pay the balance in full each month*.

If you find for whatever reason that you are simply more comfortable carrying plastic rather than cash, you should look into getting a debit card linked to your checking account. These are quite common, and in many cases, your ATM card is actually a debit card (either a Visa or MasterCard), which can be used wherever Visa and MasterCard are accepted. The debit card is used just like a credit card, but the major distinctions are that it draws funds directly from your checking account and generally is not attached to a separate line of credit. It can be handy for buying groceries and dining out, but you must remember that each time you use it, it is like you are withdrawing cash from the ATM or writing a check. Remember to balance your checkbook, and do not let your account get overdrawn through careless use of your debit card.

You may feel comforted by having one credit card around in case of emergency, in which case by all means have one. However, do not carry this card with you, making it easier for you to use it for spur of the moment splurges. Keep your credit card in a safe place and be prepared to use it only if absolutely necessary (emergency travel or medical costs, for example). Shop around for this card, in order to get the best interest rate you can, and try to get one of the credit cards linked to frequent flyer miles, which you can use for visits home or to conferences or residency interviews.

Taxes, Loans, and Other Expenses

In addition to the expenses above, you may have others particular to your situation. Perhaps you are self-employed and make quarterly tax payments, or you are making payments on student loans from college (these can usually be deferred during your medical school training; see the information on loans provided later in this chapter). You may be repaying a personal loan from another source, or perhaps you have a mortgage payment and must also pay homeowner's insurance and property taxes. You may want to purchase renter's insurance for your apartment, and you may have to make credit card payments or pay for your gym membership. You may also wish to include charitable donations and monthly savings in your budget.

Unless you are going to a local medical school, your relocation costs should figure into your budget, as well. Consider every expense you have when creating your budget, noting that some may have to be left behind—you may not have the income (or time) for a gym membership, and you may be able to use your university recreation center or a local YMCA or YWCA to save money on this expense. Perhaps you will give up on monthly savings or rent out your home if you're attending a medical school too far away to commute, as this will offset some of your home-owner expenses.

PAYING FOR IT: INTRODUCTION TO FINANCIAL AID

Unless you are independently wealthy or your family has sufficient resources to support you through your medical school career, you will need some financial assistance to supplement your own contribution to the cost of your medical education. Before you even apply to medical school, you should have your financial affairs in order. In the best of all possible situations, you will have no outstanding loans that you will need to continue paying while in medical school (car loan, personal loans, or mortgage), and you will have no credit card debt. You will not likely be able to work as a medical student; you simply will not have the time. You should try to work while in college, before you enter medical school, to pay off any existing debts. This is your first step in paying for your medical education.

> Important financial aid terms: budget, capitalization, consolidation, default, deferment, FAFSA, grace period, interest rate, principal, service-connected funds, subsidized/unsubsidized loans

Applying for Financial Aid

You should be thinking about how you will pay for medical school when you decide where to apply; cost may be a factor influencing your choices about where to apply to medical school and which school you will ultimately attend. When you have decided where you want to apply, you should contact those schools and ask for information on graduate financial aid so that you can familiarize yourself with the aid available and the application process for aid at each school. Note what forms the financial aid departments require, and be sure to list aid deadlines on your calendar. The *Medical School Admission Requirements* (MSAR) includes a table that details the forms required by each U.S. medical school, including the Free Application for Federal Student Aid (FAFSA), separate institutional forms, and supplemental application information from the student and his or her parents (MSAR 1999). It is still wise, however, to request such information directly from your schools in the event that they have changed their policies since the latest MSAR was published. International students attending medical school in the United States are ineligible for federal aid and should contact the medical schools and their financial aid departments directly to ask about financial aid available to international students as well as the application process.

If you applied for financial aid as an undergraduate, you will be familiar with the process, and you will be aware of the importance of meeting deadlines when applying for financial aid. If your financial aid application materials are not completed in a timely manner, your chances of receiving aid may be jeopardized. What little non–loan-based aid a school has available to its students may be earmarked early in the process, and if your completed financial aid applications are not received late in the spring before you plan to attend medical school, your chances of receiving any aid other than loans is quite slim. Whenever possible, get your aid applications in early. If you have information from your prospective medical schools in the fall of your senior year as an undergraduate, you will be more aware of what you need to prepare and when the information must be ready.

Previous Loans

If you received financial aid as an undergraduate, possibly including loans, you should have information on this aid at your disposal. Take the time to keep such information organized. Certainly, if you have taken student loans, you should know who owns your loans, what the amounts and interest rates are for the loans, and when repayment is to begin. If you are going into medical school directly from college, you will likely want to defer the repayment of your undergraduate loans. This is usually easy to do and requires certification that you are registered in another program for a certain number of hours (generally half- to full-time) and the processing of a deferral request form, which you must complete for your lender. This is something you should not put off until the last moment, because your repayment schedule will go into effect following a grace period, which is usually three to six months after college graduation, though some lenders require repayment to begin immediately; check the terms in your loan agreements. If you have not been granted a deferral before your first payment is due, you will have to make this and future payments until you have the deferral. Failure to make your loan payments will be defaulting on your student loans, which will not only affect your ability to be approved for future student loans, but also will damage your long-term credit.

Necessary Paperwork

All financial aid offices will require that you complete the FAFSA (see the next section), most will require a financial aid transcript from each undergraduate institution you attended, and some will have additional forms that you will need to complete before they will process your financial aid request. You should have requested information from the financial aid offices of the schools to which you applied, so that you know what forms are required and when they are due. Even if you think that you will be ineligible for most or all financial aid, or if you plan only to apply for student loans, you should complete the financial aid process at those schools you are likely to attend. This is part of the application process for government loans, your eligibility for which is determined by the financial aid office at each school, based upon the information you supply, and annual cost-of-living estimates for students attending that school.

The loan amounts for which you are eligible (and the amount you will need) will vary from school to school, depending on their budget. The budget each school uses is based on the academic year and includes tuition and fees as well as other education-related costs (books, supplies) and an estimated cost of living. It is updated yearly to reflect increased costs for tuition and other expenses and can be found in the school's catalog, usually in the section on financial aid. You may want to check with the schools to which you have applied to find out whether tuition costs are likely to increase during your attendance and also to ask what the average indebtedness is for graduates. (Tuition generally increases at a rate of approximately 5 percent each year.) Such pieces of information will help you to make a better-informed decision for your financial future.

The university will use its budget to determine your financial need, and you can use it to estimate your expenses as well, though you will have a clearer idea of your projected costs of living (using your own budget). The university budget will not include any special expenses you have, such as a car payment or credit card debt, and the school's budget includes expenses for the student only, not a spouse or children. Remember that the total of all aid you receive cannot exceed the university's budgeted amount.

Once you have completed your share of all paperwork, and all materials have been sent to your university (and your FAFSA has been completed), you must wait for the university's response. You will only receive financial aid awards from those schools to which you have been accepted. If you have responded to all requests and turned everything in on time, or even early, you can expect to hear from the schools' financial aid departments in mid-spring to late spring. If the university requires additional information, they will generally request this in writing; otherwise, you can expect to receive a financial aid award notification letter from the financial aid office detailing the funding you will receive at that school. The financial aid award generally includes aid from a variety of sources, including grants and scholarships, but the majority of your funding will likely be in the form of loans. You will probably be asked to respond to this letter, accepting or rejecting the aid package, by a certain date. *You must only accept the package from the school that you have decided to attend,* so be certain where you are going before you commit yourself to an aid package. Additional aspects of the financial aid process, as well as details on different types of aid, are discussed below.

FAFSA

The FAFSA must be filled out each year as part of your financial aid application. The FAFSA is used to determine your "need analysis" (what you can afford to contribute toward your educational costs and how much assistance you need) based on your family income and assets and your expenses. You and your parents are expected to bear the brunt of your medical school expenses, and if your parents are not able to help (or if you are independent of your parents when you apply to medical school), you will be the responsible party. If you are married, your spouse's income will be included in the sources from which you can draw funds. With this in mind, if you are married, be sure to keep your spouse informed during your application process.

This form is required by all schools if you are applying for financial aid and is necessary if you hope to qualify for any federal assistance, including federally subsidized student loans (there is more information on these later in the chapter). If you applied for aid as an undergraduate, this application will be familiar to you. It is the same form, though generally as a graduate student, you will be independent, while you may have been considered your parents' dependent as an undergraduate. What does this mean? As a dependent, your parents' income is considered by the government (and your school) when they assessed your financial need. If you are independent, only your personal income and assets (and those of your spouse) will be considered. If you are a single, independent student, this will likely make you a needier person, financially speaking; unfortunately, medical schools do not dole out a lot of grants to needy students, and your neediness may simply make your recommended subsidized loan amount greater.

Although your parental information may not be used by your financial aid office in determining your financial need, you will still need to include parental information on the FAFSA in order to qualify for any assistance from the U.S. Department of Health and Human Services. Some programs, including Scholarships for Disadvantaged Students and Primary Care Loans (PCL), require your parents' financial information, even if you are considered independent by others, such as Federal Stafford Student Loans and Health Education Assistance Loans (HEAL). It is best, in order to qualify for all types of funding, to include parental information on your FAFSA and other forms, even if you have not been supported by your family for a number of years. If you are in doubt, speak with a financial aid adviser about this distinction.

Completing the FAFSA

If you haven't filled out the FAFSA before, you can go to the FAFSA Web site (http://www.fafsa.ed.gov) to see an electronic version or to order a paper copy of the form. The FAFSA is also available at most college financial aid offices. If you filled one out last year, you should get a Renewal FAFSA in the mail by early December, but if you've moved since you last completed this form, the renewal may not find you, and you'll have start with a new form. *Don't fill out both the renewal and a new form; use one or the other.* You will be asked for your financial and educational background, and you will need to have the latest year's completed federal tax forms available to answer some of the income and asset questions. As mentioned above, your parents' financial information is also required, so you and they should try and get tax paperwork done as early as possible so that your FAFSA can be submitted in January or February of the year you are to enter medical school. If your taxes are not ready, *do not wait until April 15 to complete your FAFSA.* You can complete the FAFSA and turn it in with estimated figures, and you will then be sent an information request form so that accurate information from your tax forms is input. This must be done before the FAFSA can be completely processed, so it is best to start out with copies of your and your parents' completed tax forms on hand.

You will be asked for your educational plans, as well: what school you are likely to attend and what year of graduate school you will be in, for example. There is a question regarding other family members also attending college (thus increasing your family's economic burden). Your FAFSA will be reviewed, and you will receive a copy of your Student Aid Report (SAR) and an information review form; this is the point at which you may make any changes and/or updates. If your taxes were not complete when you first turned in your FAFSA or your address or intended schools have changed, you can update these categories now. If there were discrepancies on your FAFSA, or if required information was not supplied, you will be asked to provide new information or to review highlighted areas of your report to be sure that you made no errors. You will then have to sign and return the reviewed SAR, and a revised form will be sent to you for your files, as well as to those schools to which you applied. You can request that a copy of your SAR be sent to six schools.

Using the information on your FAFSA, your expected family contribution or student contribution will be determined. This is the amount you are expected to contribute toward your medical education. This amount, along with the amounts of any loans you are eligible to receive, will be clearly spelled out on the financial award letter you receive from the schools where you have applied for aid.

SOURCES OF FINANCIAL AID

There are many sources of financial aid for students entering medical school, including federal, national, state, local, school, and private aid. The financial aid award letter you receive from each school may include a combination of these sources, including subsidized and unsubsidized Stafford loans (explained later in the chapter), as well as any state grants for which you are eligible and departmental awards of aid, including grants and fellowships. Some of these forms of financial aid are explained below.

Free Money: Grants, Fellowships, and Scholarships

While not at all abundant, some forms of free money are offered by most medical schools in the form of institutional funds. Such funding is mainly reserved for students with financial need, though there are usually some merit-based awards as well. Only well-qualified medical students should expect to be offered merit-based funding by a medical school, so if you are not the best candidate you know, do not count on a free ride through medical school. Grant, fellowship, or scholarship money may be enough to cover the cost of tuition, though this is not always the case; sometimes the amount of the award will simply reduce the amount of tuition you must pay (from out-of-state to in-state rates, perhaps). Such awards sometimes even include a stipend intended to cover some of your living expenses, but again, such funding is scarce. To find out what is available at your chosen schools, contact the medical school and the financial aid office, and inquire about fellowship and grant monies. Many schools have funds that are reserved for particular groups of students—for example, women, members of minority groups, descendants of a family or national group, children of alumnae, or even students from particular geographic regions. You may fall into just the right category, but you'll never know unless you check into this topic carefully.

There is also free federal funding for medical students. The Medical Science Training Program (MSTP) is funded by the National Institute of General Medical Sciences and provides training leading to a combined M.D./Ph.D. degree. The program is currently available at thirty-three U.S. medical schools, with approximately 170 openings each year. Students receive up to six years of funding, which covers tuition and supplies and provides an annual stipend of $10,008. For more information on this highly competitive program, contact the MSTP administrator at the National Institutes of Health (telephone: 301-594-3830). Grants are available for Disadvantaged Health Professional Students (DHPS), and scholarships include the Exceptional Financial Need Scholarship (EFN); to qualify for this funding, you must come from a disadvantaged background and agree to practice primary-care medicine. Scholarships for Disadvantaged Students (SDS) are also available and do not require primary-care practice.

Service-connected programs are also available. The National Health Service Corps (NHSC), which is part of the U.S. Public Health Service, has a service-commitment scholarship that covers your tuition and other school expenses and also offers a monthly stipend. What's the catch? In return for this funding, you must serve as a primary-care physician in an area designated by the federal government as a health professional shortage area (HPSA). You must serve one year for each year you receive funding. (The NHSC also has a service-connected loan repayment program.) You can contact the NHSC at 800-221-9393 (toll-free). Some states have similar programs intended to provide primary or other specified care in underserved regions. These programs are usually quite competitive, and you should be certain that you are willing to live up to your end of the agreement. If you are offered such a scholarship, check the terms of the agreement carefully before you sign the contract. Military scholarships are available and are discussed below.

Other nonuniversity funds are available through states and private funders. Any scholarships or grants you receive outside of your financial aid award must be reported to your financial aid office so that your other aid can be adjusted to include the additional scholarship money. Because the school will not allow you to receive more funding than it has budgeted, an outside award will likely mean that your recommended loan amounts will be decreased. You may research nonuniversity funding on the Internet or at your local library. You may come across scholarship search services either in your library or Internet funding research; be wary of these services, which will charge you a fee for access to their database of funding. You will have to provide information on your background and plans, and the service will send you possible funding matches. Sometimes their sources are quite obvious, and there are also fraudulent search services out there. Try to do your own research before relying on one of these services.

Loans

Perhaps the most common form of financial assistance for medical students—indeed, for all graduate students—is the student loan. A loan is not to be confused with a grant or fellowship, for unlike these forms of aid, loans must be repaid by the student, who signs a promissory agreement each time he or she borrows. The cost of medical school is great, and loans may be the only way you can afford your $25,000 annual tuition as well as pay rent and buy food (once in a while). I'm sure you've heard the horror stories: it is not unusual for medical students to enter their residencies with over $100,000 in student loan debt, although in 1998 the average indebtedness for a student with loans graduating from medical school was only $85,181 (MSAR 1999). This is a heavy burden to place on your future, even if you plan to enter the most lucrative specialties in medicine. The reality is that, unless you or your family will be able to afford the tens of thousands of dollars your medical education will cost each year, you will need loans to help you get through school.

How do you qualify for a student loan, how much will you need to borrow, and where do you go for the money? This is really a very simple process, one that your medical school financial aid office will guide you through. Most loan programs require that the student be a U.S. citizen or permanent resident in compliance with Selective Service requirements and enrolled at least half-time in school. You must meet general academic requirements to continue receiving all aid (including making satisfactory progress toward a degree), you must demonstrate financial need (as indicated from the information provided on your FAFSA), and you cannot be in default on another loan.

Federal Stafford Student Loans

When you receive your financial aid award letter, it will state the loans you are being offered. Usually this a combination of Federal Stafford Student Loans, both subsidized and unsubsidized. What does this mean? Stafford loans are sponsored by the federal government, and some are actually subsidized by the federal government. This is better for you, because it means that the interest on your subsidized loans is paid by the government while you are in school, as well as during the grace period before you repay your loans and while the loans are deferred. For subsidized loans, you must meet the government's requirements for financial need. Unsubsidized Stafford loans are available to students who do not meet the requirements for subsidized loans. For Unsubsidized Stafford loans, all accrued interest is the responsibility of the borrower, who usually has the option of making interest payments while in school or having the interest on the loan capitalized. Capitalizing the interest means having the interest payments added to the principal of the loan as the payments are due. The borrower will not have to repay the interest until he or she begins repaying the loan. This will increase the amount of your payments when you do begin repaying the loan, which will be after a grace period of six to nine months after you are no longer enrolled at least half-time. Information on capitalization is usually included in the promissory note, which is the contract you sign with the lender agreeing to repay the borrowed amount, which is loaned at a certain interest rate. For Stafford loans, the interest rate is the ninety-one-day treasury bill rate plus 2.5 percent, with a current cap of 8.25 percent. Nonfederal loans will have different rates.

Federal Direct Loans

The federal government is your lender for the William D. Ford Federal Direct Student Loan Program; fewer schools participate in this program than in the Stafford loan program, so you may become more familiar with the latter. Often called the Federal Direct Loan, Ford loans are also either subsidized or unsubsidized and have the same eligibility requirements as the Stafford loan. Some schools also administer the Federal Perkins Loan Program, although this program is not always available to graduate students. Check with your financial aid office on the availability of this need-based loan program.

Selecting a Lender

Your other loans may come directly from the university or through an outside lender, which you will have to select. Your university financial aid office can advise you on reputable lenders, and often, they will send a list of lenders from which you may choose (this often means nothing more for you than filling in the name of the selected lender on the financial aid form; you may not have to contact the lender directly). Do not simply choose one of the lenders on this list based on their name or their anagram—do your research. Find out what interest rates they offer, what their grace period is, what their repayment plans are, if they offer loan consolidation, and what your deferment options are. Ask how often they capitalize interest on their loans, how long loan processing will take, and if they sell their student loans (which many lenders do). How easy it is for you to reach someone and have your questions answered is a good way for you to evaluate this lender. If you are placed on hold at length or if the customer service representative is not knowledgeable enough to answer your questions, you may want to look elsewhere for a lender. You are likely planning to borrow large sums of money over the next few years, and your relationship with this institution will extend beyond medical school and into the five years, ten years, or more that you are repaying your loans.

After you have selected your lender, you will receive an application form from them that specifies the terms of the loan, including the loan amount and interest rate. You return this form (usually to your financial aid office), and your loan is processed; if everything is in order, your loan will be guaranteed, and the funds will be provided. Many lenders use the system called Electronic Funds Transfer. For this service, which saves time, you must agree to have your loan amount electronically transferred to you university; the university will then apply these funds to your account at the university, and your unpaid tuition and fees will be paid. The remaining funds are usually issued to you in the form of a check.

Credit

If you know you have bad credit because you have defaulted on a previous loan, have filed for bankruptcy, or had problems paying your credit card bills, try to rectify this before you apply for student loans, because it can affect your chances of loan approval. This may mean you will need to wait a few years before going to medical school, or you will have to rely on less money from loans to subsidize your education. Even if you have good credit, you may want to contact a credit bureau to request a copy of your credit report. Errors frequently appear in these reports, and you should correct these errors before you complete loan applications. Not all lending agencies will do a credit check on you before approving you for a loan, but some lenders require them for unsubsidized Stafford loans, and they are also required for Health Education Assistance Loans (HEAL) and the MEDLOANS Alternative Loan Program (ALP). For credit bureau Web sites, see Appendix D.

Perhaps the financial figures on your FAFSA represent what was an extraordinarily good year for you and your family, but you have suffered a financial reversal that will affect your ability to afford medical school. This type of special situation should be discussed with a financial aid adviser, who may be able to offer an emergency loan to help you until you or your family are back on your feet. Such forms of assistance are not often advertised, so you must go looking for them. Don't give up until you have exhausted all of your options.

How Much Can You Borrow?

Quite a bit, actually. Graduate students may borrow up to $8,500 per year under the subsidized Stafford loan program (up to $65,500), and under the unsubsidized Stafford program, graduate students may borrow up to $18,500 per year (less the amount of any subsidized Stafford loan for that year, for a total Stafford debt of $138,500). These maximum amounts are updated fairly regularly, and you should contact your financial aid office for details. Of course, this is just the Stafford program; other loans are available and may be necessary for you to meet your financial needs. The Department of Health and Human Services offers need-based loans: Loans for Disadvantaged Students (LDS) and Primary Care Loans (PCL). The LDS is for students with exceptional need and has an interest rate of 5 percent. You may borrow up to the amount of your tuition plus $2,500. The PCL is for students intending to practice primary-care medicine. The PCL also has a 5 percent interest rate, provided that you practice primary care until the loan is repaid; if you do not meet this part of the agreement, your interest rate will increase to 12 percent and will be recalculated from the date you borrowed—be certain you will practice primary-care medicine before you take on this loan, and if you are unsure, look elsewhere for a loan with an interest rate under the 12 percent PCL penalty rate.

How Much Should You Borrow?

Your award letter will provide your approved loan amounts for Stafford loans, but you are not required to borrow these full amounts—you may borrow less. A loan origination fee of 3 percent is charged for Stafford loans; the bank will take this fee off the top of whatever you borrow, and the loan check you receive will reflect this charge. If you borrow $10,000, the check you receive will only be for $9,700. Plan on this fee when working out your budget and deciding how much to borrow. Keep your loan repayment schedule in mind when deciding on your loan amounts. Do not consider a student loan to be free money and borrow $10,000 more than you actually need just because it has been offered to you or so that you can live in a nicer apartment or take a winter vacation to Mexico. You will pay dearly for this in the long run. If you borrowed $20,000 this year—and that was your only loan—and you agreed on an 8 percent interest rate and to repay the loan over 10 years, your monthly loan payment would be in the neighborhood of $250. If you borrowed a more likely total of $90,000 and had the same interest rate and repayment schedule, you'll have to make payments of about $1,100 each month. This will be a large chunk of your resident's salary of approximately $35,000 per year (before taxes) and may be more than your first mortgage payment. See the tables below, Calculating Your Monthly Student Loan Payment and How Much Can You Afford to Repay, to estimate your monthly loan payments and how much you can afford to borrow.

Calculating Your Monthly Student Loan Payment
Monthly Payments for Every $1000 Borrowed

Rate	5 Years	10 Years	15 Years	20 Years	25 Years
5%	$18.87	$10.61	$ 7.91	$ 6.60	$ 5.85
8%	20.28	12.13	9.56	8.36	7.72
9%	20.76	12.67	10.14	9.00	8.39
10%	21.74	13.77	10.75	9.65	9.09
12%	22.24	14.35	12.00	11.01	10.53

*Loan factor is per $1,000; loan principal/$1,000 x loan factor = estimated monthly payment. Example: $30,000 principal borrowed at 8% on a 10 year repayment plan = $30,000/$1,000 x $12.13 = $363.90 estimated monthly payment.

How Much Can You Afford to Repay?

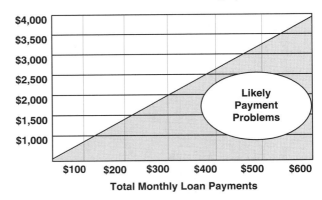

Monthly Income (after taxes) — y-axis: $4,000, $3,500, $3,000, $2,500, $2,000, $1,500, $1,000

Likely Payment Problems

Total Monthly Loan Payments — x-axis: $100, $200, $300, $400, $500, $600

If You're in over Your Head . . .

You do not want to default on your student loans; this can affect your credit, and your career, for the rest of your life. Your tax refunds may be garnished, your assets may be taken, and hospitals and licensing boards may be informed of your status. Do not jump in, sign up for loans, and plan to work out repayment details later when you're a successful physician, because payments start while you're a resident. As mentioned before, your annual salary will be near $35,000; by then, you have your loans, and it will be too late to borrow less. Your budgeting skills will be essential to you at this juncture. If you want lower payments, figure out how to borrow less money now. Suppose you decide that it would be most fulfilling for you to work in primary-care medicine in underserved areas, where your income will not be so great, but you took out over $100,000 in loans? Or say you plan to be a surgeon, and paying off your debt will be no problem, except that you do not make it into the residency you want and have to take on another specialty? Most lenders will work out special arrangements to help you repay your loans, so if you find you are having trouble meeting your payment schedule, contact your lender right away—they can report you to credit agencies if you have a payment that is sixty days past due. There are graduated payment plans that allow you to make smaller payments early in the repayment period and larger payments later on, when you are presumably going to be making a better salary. You may be able to repay your loans based on your income (which could extend the repayment period greatly). The Ford Federal Direct Loan Program offers graduated repayment and income-based repayment as well as an extended payment plan.

Consolidation

You may be able to consolidate your loans, which will simplify things for you once you've begun repayment; if you receive one loan each year, depending on the number of lenders you use, you may have to make four separate loan payments each month. A Federal Consolidation Loan will combine all of your federal loans with one lender (this loan has an interest rate that is based on an average of the loans you are consolidating), allowing you to make one monthly payment. Consolidation is not only more convenient, but your payment will likely be reduced (lengthening the repayment time for the loan up to a maximum of thirty years for $60,000 or more of consolidated debt). You may consolidate all of your federal loans or only some of them, and you can always prepay on your loans, saving yourself interest. The important thing to remember is that you will be repaying the amounts you borrow, so borrow what you need, and budget carefully to help yourself need less. The less you borrow now, the greater amount of your future income will actually be yours.

Sources of Additional Loans

If the package of loans and other aid you are offered will not meet your needs, you may need to apply for other types of non–need-based private loans or have your parents do so. The Association of American Medical Colleges (AAMC) sponsors MEDLOANS, which are only available to allopathic medical students. In addition to offering access to Federal Stafford Student Loans, MEDLOANS has an Alternative Loan Program based on the cost of attendance and the student's financial aid budget. MEDLOANS also offers MEDEX, a loan program for fourth-year medical students who need additional financial assistance as they interview and relocate for their residency program. You can get more information on MEDLOANS programs from the AAMC. The American Medical Women's Association (AMWA) Loan Program provides loans to women medical students. You can reach the AMWA at 703-838-0500. Check with your financial aid office for information on other private loans, including MedCap and MedFunds, and note that these loans will be difficult for you to obtain if you have a poor credit history. Borrowing from a family member may be another option for financing your medical education.

Service-Connected Loan Repayment

There are some medical school loans that you do not have to repay or that you will not have to repay in full, and these are usually those that have a service-connected repayment plan. The NHSC has such a plan in certain states, and the Indian Health Service (IHS) also has a loan repayment plan. The NHSC will repay up to $35,000 of student debt per year for doctors who serve in NHSC areas for two to four years. The IHS will repay up to $25,000 in student debt per year of service in an IHS location. The Federal Loan Repayment program provides payment toward student loans (up to $25,000 the first two years and $35,000 for every year thereafter), with a minimum two-year commitment in an HPSA. These service-connected loan repayment plans may sound somewhat like the military options (see the next section), but they are civilian programs and may be a very good option for many students. You may be able to make arrangements with local hospitals, which may cover some or all of the student's tuition in return for a period of service at the hospital following residency. If you work out such an arrangement, be sure to have all of the details in writing, and sign a contract specifying the amount of assistance to be provided by the hospital as well as the service you are required provide in return. You may also find, if your area of specialty is one in need, that you are offered loan repayment incentives by potential employers when you enter the job market. This is not by any means a common practice, but it is also not unheard of, so be aware of this possibility.

Military

There are several military options that will partially or completely obviate your financial needs while in medical school. While this may sound like a magical solution, the military option is definitely not for everyone and is also a very competitive route. If you are interested in military service, consider these options. The United States Army, Air Force, and Navy offer the Armed Forces Health Professions Scholarship Program (AFHPSP), which pays your tuition, fees, and other school expenses while also offering a monthly stipend for your living expenses. You must serve a year in the military for each year you are a scholarship recipient. While in school, you serve 45 days of active duty training in a hospital—you begin your military service following your residency.

The Army National Guard has the Medical Student Commissioning Program, which commissions students already in medical school as second lieutenants in the Medical Services Corps (with a promotion to captain upon graduation). This option requires 16 hours of training per month and an additional two weeks of training per year. The Department of Defense also has an assistance program, under which the student is on inactive duty in the Medical Corps reserves. Educational expenses are paid, and stipends are provided while the student participates in their residency program. For the first year of residency, two years of active service are required; then a half year of service is required for each additional half year of residency supported. In addition to the active service, an eight-year reserve service commission is required.

These are very competitive scholarships, and you will need to apply for them while still in college. Be certain that the military option is for you before you decide on this, however. For more information, you can contact your local Army, Air Force, or Navy recruiting office.

Another military option is the Uniformed Services University of the Health Sciences F. Edward Hébert School of Medicine. This is the U.S. government medical school, located on the grounds of the

Naval Hospital in Bethesda, Maryland. As with the government's universities (the U.S. Naval Academy, West Point, etc.), the application process for this school is quite rigorous. Also like those schools, the intent of the Uniformed Services University is to prepare you for a career as a military (medical) officer. Thus, you will receive not only a medical education, but also a military orientation and background in specific aspects of military medicine.

You must be between the ages of 18 and 30 to be accepted to this school and must also meet the physical requirements of the armed forces. You shouldn't expect to get into this school just because you are a good candidate for medical school; because they want to train future military officers, the admission personnel want candidates who know something about the military and can express a genuine interest in a military career. If you are accepted and choose to attend this school, you will be commissioned into the military (as a second lieutenant in the Army or Air Force or an ensign in the Navy) and will receive military pay and benefits. You can expect a promotion to captain (Army and Air Force) or lieutenant (Navy) when you receive your M.D. You will be on active duty in the service for the duration of your medical education. After your education is complete, you will owe the armed forces seven years of active military service as a medical officer, followed by six years of reserve service (time in internships or residencies do not count toward this duty).

This sounds like a big commitment, and it is, but your medical education is completely paid for. As with the other military options, you will serve as a military doctor and will not be starting at the bottom of the ranks. You will be paid for your time in the service, as all military personnel are, and your military service will be considered compensation for your completely free medical training. If you think about it, this is a pretty good deal. While many new doctors are struggling to make their student loan payments and eat, you will be making a living as a medical doctor, free of debt. You may even find yourself stationed in some interesting locale, such as Hawaii or

Germany. However, you will be in the U.S. military, and if a plastic surgery practice in Beverly Hills is where you want to be, consider that you will have to wait a long time to get that career started. You may also wind up in Yuma, Arizona, or Bosnia for a while. If you enter this school and decide it's not for you, or you cannot handle the military aspect of the school, you may be required to serve active duty time equal to the length of time you were in the program (minimum one year) or to reimburse the federal government for tuition and fees. For some this may be the perfect option—just be sure before you sign up.

Aid for Members of Minority Groups

Students who are underrepresented in the medical fields include African Americans, Native Americans (American Indians, Alaskan Natives, and Native Hawaiians), Mexican Americans, and mainland Puerto Ricans. The AAMC designated these groups underrepresented in medicine more than twenty years ago, and they remain so today. Most scholarship money is reserved for students with financial need, but minority students will find some sources of financial assistance for medical students that are earmarked for members of minority groups only, and many colleges have such funding at their disposal that they use to help them recruit minority medical students. The financial barrier can be great for all students, and funding for members of minority groups is generally provided with the aim of increasing the numbers of these students in medical school by alleviating this barrier, which keeps larger numbers of minority students from applying or attending. Some forms of assistance also create an incentive for more of these students to apply to medical school. The AAMC launched their Project 3000 by 2000 in 1991; this project is intended to increase the number of minority students entering medical school each year to 3,000 by the year 2000. In 1998, members of minority groups comprised only 11.6 percent (1,872 students) of the entering class (MSAR 1999)—the AAMC is still a long way from its goal.

The Indian Health Service Scholarship, which covers tuition and fees and includes a monthly stipend, is available for Native American and Native Alaskan students. This is a service-connected award, and recipients have a two-year-minimum service agreement. For more information, contact the Indian Health Service Scholarship Program (telephone: 301-443-6197).

When considering to which medical schools you should apply, be sure to check on the availability of aid to members of underrepresented groups at different universities. For more information on the sources of minority aid available, contact financial aid offices at the medical schools to which you are applying. Low-interest loans may also be available for minority students. Most universities have an office of minority affairs; also contact these departments for information on minority recruitment policies and available funding for minority students. If the colleges you are interested in do not have minority affairs offices, inquire about minority programs at the student affairs office.

Teaching/Research Assistantships

A teaching or research assistantship is a paid position that may or may not include a full or partial tuition waiver. Assistantships normally require twenty or fewer hours of work weekly, and duties may include grading papers, assisting faculty members with mundane office chores (photocopying or filing), and even leading or supervising small group or lab sessions that are a required part of a larger lecture course. Assistantships are more common in other graduate programs (the social sciences and humanities), where they constitute the bulk of merit-based student financial aid offered by the department.

Within medical programs, assistantships are less common, perhaps because medical programs are so time-consuming to begin with. Medical students can sometimes get an assistantship with a professor in whose course they do particularly well. If you ace anatomy, for example, in your second or third year, you may be able to work for the professor in an assistantship capacity. An assistantship is normally guaranteed for one year, but is generally renewable (as are other forms of assistance), pending academic and work performance.

If All Else Fails

If you are unable to secure the aid you need to pay for your medical education, check into other payment options at your chosen school. Some have emergency loan programs, and monthly payment plans are also available that may ease the strain of paying your bill in only two parts, once each semester. Your school may not offer such programs, but you never know unless you ask.

"I ended up choosing UC–San Diego for several reasons. Having been raised on the East Coast, I had always had a desire to spend some time on the West Coast. The cost was significantly cheaper than a private medical school on the East Coast (I was deciding between Columbia, Penn, UC–San Diego, and University of Virginia). And, at the time, UCSD had quite a reputation as an 'up and coming' medical school."

—former medical student, University of California, San Diego, School of Medicine

---

WHERE TO GO?

You know where you have been accepted and you have your financial aid offers, so now you can decide which school to attend. Unless you are very lucky and your first-choice school has accepted you and offered you a wonderful aid package, this will be a difficult time. You may find that the school that was once at the top of your list has fallen to third place. Why? Because you got better financial aid offers from two other schools. Certainly, cost should not be the only factor influencing your choice of school, but hardly anyone can deny that it is a factor. If you are offered a grant that covers tuition costs at your number three school and your number two school offers you a $50,000 loan package, it may be very difficult to resist the free tuition.

You will have to weigh the differences that made you rate the schools as you did to begin with—why was Columbia your first choice and Harvard your third? You may find that you still want to attend your first choice and will do so, even if it means a lot of loans, or you may decide that the differences between the schools are negligible or that the financial award from your third choice really does matter enough to move it up in your estimation. These are very difficult categories to weigh, and the decision is a personal one. Be sure to make this choice carefully—do not accept your first-choice offer of admission before you know what their award package will be, and do not accept the award package from your third choice until you have heard from the financial aid offices of the other schools to which you have been accepted.

A FINAL WORD ON BUDGETS

You know where you're going and how much it will cost, you've applied for your student loans, and you know how much you will be receiving just before the fall semester. This is where your budgeting know-how will really come in to play: you now can calculate you income and expenses and give yourself a real budget. If you know how much money you will get from your student loans, say $15,000 each semester, and you know that $8,000 will go directly to your school to cover your tuition and fees, you know that you have $6,550 (don't forget the origination fee for the lender) to get you through the semester, covering all your other expenses. Finalize your budget using this figure: if school starts in August and your next loan check arrives in January, you will need to make this money last about five months. That's a monthly budget of $1,310. This is all the money you will have, so go through your list of expenses and adjust the figures until you are spending no more than the amount you have each month ($1,310). Do not allow yourself to run out of money in November!

Once You're There

Chapter 6

ADJUSTING

Is medical school going to be just like college? No. Most medical students say that medical school is a lot more intense than college. You will likely be under a great deal of stress and pressure to perform well, even if you go to a relatively noncompetitive school. Your classmates will be among the brightest students to graduate college, and many high-achieving students put pressure on themselves to achieve, even if they are not competing with other students. Your medical school class may be a very diverse group with very different backgrounds and interests, but you have all entered this program with the same goal in mind: you want to become medical doctors. In your first two years, you will have to do a lot of memorizing, which is very difficult for many students. Your third and fourth years will be filled with clinical study (and exams), and you may find yourself with little or no free time. These are generalizations, of course, and for a better idea of life at a particular school, try to speak with students there, or see Peterson's *The Insider's Guide to Medical Schools*, which is written by medical students.

> "Medical school is much more work than college. No more 'let's learn this because it's cool.' Instead, you have to know this or you'll kill someone."
>
> —former medical student, University of Texas Southwestern Medical Center at Dallas

COURSES (AND THE TRIED-AND-TRUE METHODS OF GETTING THROUGH THEM)

Though this is not the case everywhere, at most schools your first two years will be filled with lectures and labs in which you are taught the foundations of your medical education. These courses will prepare you for the first of your U.S. Medical Licensing Examinations (USMLE), which you take after your second year of medical school and for which most medical schools will require a passing grade. It is important to get all you can from these years of study. As with the MCAT, your course notes will be useful study guides.

If you are not a competitive person, you may not feel the pressure do extremely well and stay ahead of your medical school peers. It is likely, though, that as you have made it into medical school, you are competitive and like to do well. You will find students of all types in medical school, including highly competitive students, who seem more interested in being the best than in learning medicine; model students, who carry filofaxes, study their copious class notes every evening, and meet with their professors weekly to discuss their progress and ask any questions not handled in class; and students who never seem to study or go to class but somehow manage to squeak by. You are probably a mix of these stereotypes: you like to do well, but it's not the most important thing; you are organized and study and complete course work on time; and you also know when it's time to give yourself a break from studying.

If you find yourself leaning too much toward any of these stereotypes, you may want to take stock of your situation and try to get some help from your academic adviser or a student counselor. Will you respond to the pressure of medical school by making yourself a hermit and a control freak who is unable to appreciate new information but committing it all to memory without meaning in order to get a good grade? Will you obsess about all of the details, planning your study schedule and hyperorganizing your notes but not really enjoying it and not meeting anyone outside of class? Will you be in over your head after the first few weeks of class, unable to catch up in anatomy and unable even to remember where your physiology class meets? These are ways in which students deal with stress: some force themselves to excel, some organize the problems, and others go into avoidance. If you can maintain a balance, you'll be able to learn what you need in the first two years while also appreciating what the material will mean to your future in medicine. You may even make some friends along the way. Of course you want to do well, but a good doctor is a humane person. Don't lose touch with why you are studying medicine: you want to help others.

> "Medical school wasn't intellectually difficult but the amount of material and minutiae we're required to know can get to you. One simile I heard which I believe is accurate is it's like trying to get a drink of water from an open fire hydrant. The type of learning involved in medical school was rote memorization. . . . Also, the pace of medical school versus college is very different. I'd say a college course covers in a semester what a medical school course covers in six to eight weeks."
>
> —Dr. Sachin Shah, former medical student, Villanova–MCP Hahnemann University accelerated program

CLINICAL STUDY

Your third and fourth years will likely take you into clinical study, which may be what you've been looking forward to. (At some schools, clinical study begins before the third year.) You will have the opportunity to work hands-on with patients. At last, you will see the importance of all of the memorization and studying you had to do in your first two years of medical school. If you put pressure on yourself in your classes, you may be overwhelmed at this point, because this is the stage of your medical training at which the importance of the doctor's role will strike home. It's no longer about memorization; it's now about patient care. You will be required to do a series of six- to twelve-week clinical clerkships in particular areas of medicine, usually including medicine, primary care, surgery, pediatrics, obstetrics, and psychiatry. Additional courses, preceptorships, and a number of clinical elective clerkships may also be required in your final year.

By your third and fourth years, while you are doing your clerkships, you should start thinking ahead to your residency, considering what specialty you would like to study further—a decision your clerkships should help you make. Your residency will determine the type of medicine you practice. This is not a decision to be made lightly. As mentioned earlier in this volume, the medical school you attend to some extent determines what type of residency you are likely to receive. If you think you want to go into neurological medicine, be sure that the school you choose to attend offers a clerkship in this area. If you finish school with no experience at all in the area of the residency you are seeking, you are unlikely to match for that residency.

The difficulty of the school you attend is also considered when residency matches are made, so if you attend a school that is not as academically rigorous as some others, you must try to do very well in your courses. Experience in your area of interest outside of medical school may also help make you a more competitive residency candidate. Rather than taking summers off to travel or lifeguarding at a local pool, look for internships in the area in which you want to specialize, obstetrics for example, or volunteer on a research project on obstetrics being conducted at your school or one of its affiliated institutions.

When selecting your residency preference, you should consider not only how well qualified you are for the residency, but also how the residency will benefit you. Currently there is a surplus of doctors in the U.S., and in some specialties, the surplus is decidedly worse than in others. Make sure you are not adding to the glut (and thereby lessening your chances of being gainfully employed practicing medicine in your area of specialty) when you decide on your specialization. Some areas of medicine—geriatrics, for example—are actually growing, and if you have an interest in one of them, so much the better. Look into the viability of your area of interest before you commit yourself to this career path.

Becoming a Doctor

Soon you will be a doctor, and others will rely on you to diagnose and treat their illnesses. This is a position of huge responsibility, so learn all you can during your training. You may not be exposed to training in bedside manner, but you should remember how important this is: patients want a doctor they feel confident in, but also one who is caring and interested in them as people, not merely as medical cases. You should be learning from your patients as well as from your supervisors.

> "The average resident makes between $30,000 and $40,000 per year, working 100-hour weeks, for three to eight years. Loan repayment takes up the bulk of our incomes, until we finally become board-licensed physicians."
>
> —resident and former medical student, University of California, San Diego, School of Medicine

STRESS (AND RELEASE)

As important as it is to work hard and do well in medical school, relaxation can sometimes be just as important. Make sure you have some nonacademic outlets, such as sports or other activities and hobbies. Activities that do not require huge investments of time and money are perhaps best. Maybe you enjoy walking or reading, or perhaps yoga or chess is relaxing for you. If the activity that you most enjoy is water skiing and you are attending medical school in North Dakota, you would need a weeklong vacation to squeeze in your relaxation, and this will not be practical. If water is the key, try to satisfy yourself with swimming at the campus recreation center. You should be able to find a way to fit a relaxing hobby into your hectic medical student life, if only for a few hours each week. Decompression time is important, and physical activity is not only good for your body, but also for your mind. You may find that the answer to the problem you have been grappling with comes into focus while you are running, when your mind is clear. Even is this isn't the case, the physical activity should help you think and sleep better, and if your sleep time is restricted, the quality of your rest will be very important.

Social Life

One important outlet can be your social life. You may not have time for much of one, but if you can squeeze in your favorite social activity once in a while—dancing with friends, a trip to the movies or theater, or dining out with some other students—you will find it a welcome release from the stresses of medical school. Just taking a few hours, not only to commiserate with your friends about how school is going and how impossible a particular professor is but also to forget about school, make new friends, and learn about the people you study with, can reenergize you for days to come. Money will likely be an issue for you, as it is with most graduate students, but there are many ways to be social on a budget. Rent movies rather than going to a theater and arrange a potluck rather than heading to an expensive restaurant. You may find that the time away from your studies spent enjoying the company of others is much more important than what movie you see or where you eat. You should be able to fit an activity like this into your schedule every few weeks—it will only take a few hours—and you should try to do so. You'll be glad you did, and your friends will thank you as well.

WORDS OF ADVICE

If you are afraid of what you'll find when you get to your chosen medical school, you haven't done your research well. By the time you have chosen the school you will attend, you should have visited at least once when you had your interview. If you took full advantage of this visit, you spoke not only with your interviewer, but also with faculty members and administrators as well as students. You had a tour of the medical school facilities and asked the questions that helped you select this school over the others that accepted you. Even before the interview stage, you researched this school, read the catalog, browsed the Web site, and contacted student representatives via e-mail for firsthand student experiences of the school. You know what the goals of the school are, what its curriculum entails, what clerkships are required and offered, and what other special opportunities the school has to offer. You should have a great deal of information at your disposal on the school you are about to attend. Of course, you will be nervous before your first day of medical school, as you likely were when you entered your first college classroom. But this should be an exciting unknown rather than a frightening one. Your medical career begins with your first day at your medical school, and it should be a long career. When things get rough, remind yourself of the reasons you underwent the grueling admission process to begin with. You made it into medical school, and your chances of graduating are much greater than your chances of acceptance were. So look to the future. The adventure begins here.

Medical Schools and Their Affiliated Hospitals

Appendix A

ALLOPATHIC SCHOOLS

Refer to current catalog if no clinical affiliations are listed.

Alabama

University of Alabama School of Medicine
Birmingham, Alabama
Telephone: 205-934-2330
E-mail: admissions@uasom.meis.uab.edu
Web site: http://www.uab.edu/uasom/

University of South Alabama College of Medicine
Mobile, Alabama
Telephone: 334-460-7176
Web site: http://southmed.usouthal.edu/index.html

University of South Alabama Medical Center, Searcy Hospital, U.S.A. Cancer Center, U.S.A. Children's and Women's Hospitals

Arizona

University of Arizona College of Medicine
Tucson, Arizona
Telephone: 520-626-6214

Web site: http://www.medicine.arizona.edu

University Medical Center, Children's Research Center, Arizona Cancer Center

Arkansas

University of Arkansas College of Medicine

Little Rock, Arkansas
Telephone: 501-686-5354
E-mail: southtomg@exchange.uams.edu
Web site: http://www.uams.edu

University Hospital, Arkansas Cancer Research Center, Harvey and Bernice Jones Eye Institute, Donald W. Reynolds Center on Aging

California

Keck School of Medicine of the University of Southern California

Los Angeles, California
Telephone: 323-442-2552
E-mail: medadmit@hsc.usc.edu
Web site: http://www.usc.edu/keck

Los Angeles County USC Medical Center, USC University Hospital, USC/Norris Cancer Center and Hospital, Doheny Eye Institute, Children's Hospital Los Angeles, Rancho Los Amigos Medical Center, Orthopedic Hospital, Hospital of the Good Samaritan, Barlow Respiratory Hospital, California Medical Center, Huntington Memorial Hospital, Presbyterian Intercommunity Hospital, House Ear Institute, Veterans Administration Outpatient Clinic, White Memorial Medical Center

Loma Linda University School of Medicine

Loma Linda, California
Telephone: 909-824-4467
Web site: http://www.llu.edu

LLU Medical Center, Children's Hospital, LLU Community Medical

Center, Loma Linda Behavioral Medicine Center, Jerry L. Pettis Memorial Veterans Hospital, Riverside County Regional Medical Center, White Memorial Medical Center, San Bernardino County General Hospital, Kaiser Foundation Hospital, Glendale Adventist Medical Center

Stanford University School of Medicine
Stanford, California
Telephone: 415-723-6861
Web site: http://www.stanford.edu

University Hospital, Lucile Packard Children's Hospital, Santa Clara County Valley Medical Center, Palo Alto Veterans Administration Hospital

University of California, Davis, School of Medicine
Davis, California
Telephone: 530-752-2717
Web site: http://www-med.ucdavis.edu/

University Medical Center, Shriners Hospital for Children, Ellison Ambulatory Care Center

University of California, Irvine, College of Medicine
Irvine, California
Telephone: 949-824-5388 or 800-824-5388 (toll-free)
Web site: http//www.com.uci.edu

UCI Medical Center, numerous affiliated hospitals and clinics

University of California, Los Angeles, School of Medicine
Los Angeles, California
Telephone: 310-825-6081
Web site: http://www.medsch.ucla.edu/admiss/

University Medical Center, UCLA Ambulatory Medical Plaza, UCLA Children's Hospital, Stein Eye Institute, Los Angeles County Harbor/ UCLA Medical Center, Veterans Administration Medical Centers at West Los Angeles and Sepulveda, Cedars–Sinai Medical Center, Olive View Medical Center, Santa Monica Hospital

University of California, San Diego, School of Medicine
La Jolla, California
Telephone: 619-534-3880
Web site: http://www.medicine.ucsd.edu

UC Medical Center, Veterans Administration Hospital, Naval Regional
Medical Center, eight affiliated hospitals and clinics

University of California, San Francisco, School of Medicine
San Francisco, California
Telephone: 415-476-4044
Web site: http://www.som.ucsf.edu

Colorado

University of Colorado School of Medicine
Denver, Colorado
Telephone: 303-315-7361
Web site: http://www.uchsc.edu

Affiliated hospitals and clinics throughout the Denver area

Connecticut

University of Connecticut School of Medicine
Farmington, Connecticut
Telephone: 860-679-4713
E-mail: sanford@nso1.uchc.edu
Web site: http://www.uchc.edu

University Hospital and Ambulatory Unit, eight affiliated hospitals in the
greater Hartford area, eleven allied community hospitals

Yale University School of Medicine
New Haven, Connecticut
Telephone: 203-785-2643
E-mail: medicalschool.admissions@quickmail.yale.edu
Web site: http://info.med.yale.edu/medadmit

*Yale–New Haven Hospital, West Haven Veterans Hospital, Connecticut
Mental Health Center, Yale Psychiatric Institute, Hospital of St. Raphael,
Waterbury Hospital*

District of Columbia

Georgetown University School of Medicine
Washington, D.C.
Telephone: 202-687-1154
Web site: http://www.dml.georgetown.edu/schmed

*University Hospital, Concentrated Care Center, Outpatient Surgical Cen-
ter, Vincent T. Lombardi Cancer Research Center, nine affiliated federal
and community hospitals in the Washington metropolitan area*

George Washington University School of Medicine and Health Sciences
Washington, D.C.
Telephone: 202-994-3506
E-mail: medadmit@gwis2.circ.gwu.edu
Web site: http://www.gwumc.edu/edu/admis

*University Hospital and clinics, Children's National Medical Center,
Fairfax Hospital, Holy Cross Hospital, National Naval Medical Center,
St. Elizabeth's Hospital, Veterans Administration Hospital, Washington
Hospital Center*

Howard University College of Medicine
Washington, D.C.
Telephone: 202-806-6270
Web site: http://www.med.howard.edu

*University Hospital, District of Columbia General Hospital, St. Eliza-
beth's Hospital, Walter Reed Army Medical Center, U.S. Naval Medical
Center, Washington Veterans Administration Medical Center, Providence
Hospital, National Rehabilitation Hospital, Washington Hospital Center,
Prince George's Hospital Center*

Florida

University of Florida College of Medicine
Gainesville, Florida
Telephone: 352-392-4569
Web site: http://www.med.ufl.edu

Shands Hospital, Brain Institute, Veterans Administration Medical Center, University of Florida Health Science Center–Jacksonville, affiliations in Ft. Lauderdale, Miami, Orlando, and Pensacola

University of Miami School of Medicine
Miami, Florida
Telephone: 305-243-6791
E-mail: med.admissions@miami.edu
Web site: http://www.miami.edu/medical-admissions

Jackson Memorial Hospital, Veterans Affairs Medical Center, Mailman Center for Child Development, Bascom Palmer Eye Institute and Anne Bates Leach Eye Hospital, Applebaum Magnetic Resonance Imaging Center, Ambulatory Care Center, UM Hospitals and Clinics, Diabetes Research Institute, Ryder Trauma Center, Sylvester Comprehensive Cancer Center

University of South Florida College of Medicine
Tampa, Florida
Telephone: 813-974-2229
Web site: http://www.med.usf.edu

USF Medical Clinics, Tampa General Hospital, James A. Haley Veterans Hospital, Tampa Unit Shriners Hospital for Crippled Children, H. Lee Moffitt Cancer Center and Research Institute, University Psychiatry Center, University Diagnostic Institute, Genesis Clinic, USF Eye Institute, USF Dialysis Center, 17 Davis Pediatric Ambulatory Care Center, All Children's Hospital, Bayfront Medical Center, Bay Pines Veterans Hospital, Orlando Regional Medical Center

Georgia

Emory University School of Medicine

Atlanta, Georgia
Telephone: 404-727-5660
E-mail: medschadmiss@medadm.emory.edu
Web site: http://www.emory.edu/WHSC

Medical College of Georgia School of Medicine

Augusta, Georgia
Telephone: 706-721-3186
E-mail: sclmed.stadmin@mail.mcg.edu
Web site: http://www.mcg.edu

Medical College of Georgia Hospital and Clinics, affiliated hospitals in Augusta and cities throughout the state

Mercer University School of Medicine

Macon, Georgia
Telephone: 912-752-2524
E-mail: kothanek.j@gain.mercer.edu
Web site: http://www.mercer.edu

Mercer Health Systems, Medical Center of Central Georgia, Memorial Medical Center, Floyd Medical Center, Phoebe Putney Memorial Hospital, Medical Center in Columbus, several rural hospitals throughout the state

Morehouse School of Medicine

Atlanta, Georgia
Telephone: 404-752-1650
Web site: http://www.msm.edu

Grady Memorial Hospital, Southwest Community Hospital, Tuskegee Veterans Administration Medical Center, Area Health Education Center Program

Hawaii

University of Hawaii at Manoa John A. Burns School of Medicine

Honolulu, Hawaii

Telephone: 808-956-8300

E-mail: nishikim@jabsom.biomed.hawaii.edu

Web site: http://medworld.biomed.hawaii.edu

Leahi Hospital, affiliated community hospitals and primary-care clinics throughout the state

Illinois

Finch University of Health Sciences/Chicago Medical School

North Chicago, Illinois

Telephone: 847-578-3206

E-mail: jonesk@mis.finchcms.edu

Web site: http://www.finchcms.edu

Cook County Hospital, Edward Hines Veterans Affairs Medical Center, Illinois Masonic Medical Center, Swedish Covenant Hospital, Norwalk Hospital, Lutheran General Hospital

Loyola University of Chicago Stritch School of Medicine

Maywood, Illinois

Telephone: 708-216-3229

Web site: http://www.meddean.luc.edu

Foster G. McGaw Hospital, Hines Veterans Administration Hospital, affiliated hospitals in the Chicago area

Northwestern University Medical School

Chicago, Illinois

Telephone: 312-503-8206

E-mail: med-admissions@nwu.edu

Web site: http://www.nums.nwu.edu/viewbook/mdprog.htm

McGaw Hospitals: Northwestern Memorial, Children's Memorial, Evanston, and Glenbrook; Rehabilitation Institute of Chicago; VA Chicago Health Care System–Lakeside Division

Rush Medical College of Rush University

Chicago, Illinois

Telephone: 312-942-6913

Web site: http://www.rushu.rush.edu/medcol

Rush–Presbyterian–St. Luke's Medical Center, affiliated hospitals and neighborhood health center

Southern Illinois University School of Medicine

Springfield, Illinois

Telephone: 217-524-6013

Web site: http://www.siumed.edu

University Medical Center

University of Chicago Pritzker School of Medicine

Chicago, Illinois

Telephone: 773-702-1937

Web site: http://pritzker.bsd.uchicago.edu

University Hospitals, Weiss Hospital, MacNeal Hospital, Jules Knapp Institute for Molecular Medicine

University of Illinois at Chicago College of Medicine

Chicago, Illinois

Telephone: 312-996-5635

Web site: http://www.uic.edu/depts/mcam

Indiana

Indiana University School of Medicine

Indianapolis, Indiana

Telephone: 317-274-3772

Web site: http://www.iupui.edu/it/medschl/home.html

University Hospitals, three affiliated hospitals

Iowa

University of Iowa College of Medicine

Iowa City, Iowa

Telephone: 319-335-8052

E-mail: medical-admissions@uiowa.edu

Web site: http://www.medicine.uiowa.edu/osac/osac.htm

University Hospitals and Clinics, Veterans Administration

Kansas

University of Kansas School of Medicine

Kansas City, Kansas

Telephone: 913-588-5245

Web site: http://www.kumc.edu/som/som.html

University Hospital, four affiliated Wichita hospitals

Kentucky

University of Kentucky College of Medicine

Lexington, Kentucky

Telephone: 606-323-6161

Web site: http://www.comed.uky.edu/medicine

University Hospital, Veterans Affairs Medical Center, Kentucky Clinic, affiliated hospitals in Lexington and throughout the state

University of Louisville School of Medicine

Louisville, Kentucky

Telephone: 502-852-5193

Web site: http://www.louisville.edu

University Hospital, Kosair–Children's Hospital, Jewish Hospital, Norton Hospital, Veterans Administration Medical Center, Kentucky Lions Eye Research Institute, James Brown Cancer Center, Child Evaluation Center, Amelia Brown Frazier Rehabilitation Center, Trover Clinic

Louisiana

Louisiana State University School of Medicine in New Orleans

New Orleans, Louisiana

Telephone: 504-568-6262

E-mail: ms-admissions@lsumc.edu

Web site: http://www.medschool.lsumc.edu/admissions

*University Hospital, Medical Center of Louisiana in New Orleans, Lions–
LSU Clinics, University Medical Center Lafayette, Earl K. Long Hospital,
affiliated hospitals in New Orleans*

Louisiana State University School of Medicine in Shreveport

Shreveport, Louisiana

Telephone: 318-675-5190

E-mail: shvadm@lsumc.edu

Web site: http://lib-sh.lsumc.edu

*University Hospital and Clinics, Shreveport Veterans Administration
Hospital*

Tulane University School of Medicine

New Orleans, Louisiana

Telephone: 504-588-5187

E-mail: medsch@tmcpop.tmc.tulane.edu

Web site: http://www.mcl.tulane.edu

*Charity Hospital of New Orleans, Veterans Affairs Medical Center, Tulane
Medical Center Hospital and Clinic, Tulane Hospital for Children, affiliated hospitals and clinics in New Orleans and other communities*

Maryland

Johns Hopkins University School of Medicine

Baltimore, Maryland

Telephone: 410-955-3182

Web site: http://www.med.jhu.edu/admissions

*Johns Hopkins Hospital, Outpatient Center, Kennedy Krieger Institute,
affiliated centers*

Uniformed Services University of the Health Sciences F. Edward Hébert School of Medicine

Bethesda, Maryland

Telephone: 301-295-3101 or 800-772-1743 (toll-free)

Web site: http://www.usuhs.mil

Bethesda Naval Hospital, associated federal health resources in the greater Washington metropolitan area

University of Maryland School of Medicine

Baltimore, Maryland

Telephone: 410-706-7478

Web site: http://www.som1.ab.umd.edu

University Medical System, affiliated hospitals in the Baltimore area

Massachusetts

Boston University School of Medicine

Boston, Massachusetts

Telephone: 617-638-4630

Web site: http://www.bumc.bu.edu

University Hospital, twenty-one affiliated health care facilities

Harvard Medical School

Boston, Massachusetts

Telephone: 617-432-1550

E-mail: admissions_office@hms.harvard.edu

Web site: http://www.hms.harvard.edu

Massachusetts General Hospital, Brigham and Women's Hospital, Children's Hospital, Beth Israel Deaconess Medical Center, Massachusetts Eye and Ear Hospital, Mount Auburn Hospital, Cambridge Hospital, Massachusetts Mental Health Center, McLean Hospital, West Roxbury and Brockton VA Medical Centers, Shriners Burns Institute, Spaulding Rehabilitation Hospital, Harvard Vanguard Medical Associates

Tufts University School of Medicine

Boston, Massachusetts

Telephone: 617-636-6571

Web site: http://tufts.edu/med

More than thirty affiliated hospitals

University of Massachusetts Medical School

Worcester, Massachusetts

Telephone: 508-856-2323

E-mail: anne.parlante@umassmed.edu

Web site: http://www.ummed.edu/dept/med_school_admissions/admissions.html

UMass Memorial Medical Center, affiliated regional community hospitals and health centers, Massachusetts Biotechnology Research Park

Michigan

Michigan State University College of Human Medicine

East Lansing, Michigan

Telephone: 517-353-9620

E-mail: mdadmissions@msu.edu

Web site: http://www.chm.msu.edu

University of Michigan Medical School

Ann Arbor, Michigan

Telephone: 734-764-6317

Web site: http://www.med.umich.edu/medschool

University Hospitals, St. Joseph Mercy Hospital, Veterans Administration Hospital, Oakwood Hospital and Clinics, William Beaumont Hospital

Wayne State University School of Medicine

Detroit, Michigan

Telephone: 313-577-1466

Web site: http://www.med.wayne.edu

Detroit Medical Center Hospitals, Sinai Hospital, St. John Hospital, William Beaumont Hospital, Oakwood Hospital, Providence Hospital, and St. Joseph Mercy Hospital

Minnesota

Mayo Medical School

Rochester, Minnesota

Telephone: 507-284-3671

Web site: http://www.mayo.edu/education/mms/MMS_home_page.
html

Mayo Clinic, four affiliated hospitals, primary-care facilities, including several rural clinics

University of Minnesota, Duluth, School of Medicine
Duluth, Minnesota
Telephone: 218-726-8511
E-mail: jcarls10@d.umn.edu
Web site: http://www.d.umn.edu/medWeb/admissions

St. Mary's/Duluth Clinic, Miller-Dwan Medical Center, St. Luke's Hospital of Duluth

University of Minnesota Medical School–Minneapolis
Minneapolis, Minnesota
Telephone: 612-624-1122
E-mail: galva001@ maroon.tc.umn.edu
Web site: http://www.med.umn.edu

Most major hospitals in the Minneapolis–St. Paul area

Mississippi

University of Mississippi School of Medicine
Jackson, Mississippi
Telephone: 601-984-5010
Web site: http://www.umsmed.edu

University Hospital, Blair E. Batson Children's Hospital, Veterans Administration Hospital, McBryde Rehabilitation Center for the Blind

Missouri

Saint Louis University School of Medicine
St. Louis, Missouri
Telephone: 314-577-8205
E-mail: mcpeters@slu.edu
Web site: http://www.slu.edu/colleges/med

University Hospital, David P. Wohl Memorial Mental Health Institute, Cardinal Glennon Hospital for Children, SLU–Anheuser Busch Eye Institute, Institute of Molecular Virology, Deaconess Medical Center, DePaul Medical Center, St. John's Mercy Medical Center, St. Mary's Health Center, St. Louis Veterans Administration Hospitals

University of Missouri–Columbia School of Medicine

Columbia, Missouri
Telephone: 573-882-2923
E-mail: nolkej@health.missouri.edu
Web site: http://www.hsc.missouri.edu/cares

University Hospital and Clinics, Mid-Missouri Mental Health Center, Harry S. Truman Veterans Administration Hospital, Howard A. Rusk Rehabilitation Center, Cosmopolitan International Diabetes Center, Ellis-Fischel Cancer Center, Green Meadows Clinic, Crossroads West Clinic, Fairview clinic, rural primary-care clinics

University of Missouri–Kansas City School of Medicine

Kansas City, Missouri
Telephone: 816-235-1870
Web site: http://research.med.umkc.edu

Affiliated community hospitals

Washington University School of Medicine

St. Louis, Missouri
Telephone: 314-362-6857
E-mail: wumscoa@msnotes.wustl.edu
Web site: http://medschool.wustl.edu/admissions

Barnes-Jewish Hospital, St. Louis Children's Hospital, Barnard Hospital, Central Institute for the Deaf

Nebraska

Creighton University School of Medicine

Omaha, Nebraska
Telephone: 402-280-2799
E-mail: medschadm@creighton.edu

Web site: http://www.creighton.edu

St. Joseph's Hospital, Children's Memorial Hospital, Veterans Administration Hospital, Alegent Health System Hospital, several other area hospitals

University of Nebraska College of Medicine
Omaha, Nebraska
Telephone: 402-559-2259
Web site: http://www.unmc.edu/UNCOM/index.html

Nebraska Health System Hospitals, University Outpatient Services, University Geriatric Center, Eppley Cancer Research Institute, C. Loius Meyer Children's Rehabilitation Institute, Veterans Affairs Hospital, eight private hospitals

Nevada

University of Nevada School of Medicine
Reno, Nevada
Telephone: 775-784-6063
E-mail: asa@unr.edu
Web site: http://www.unr.edu/unr/med.html

Affiliated community health facilities

New Hampshire

Dartmouth Medical School
Hanover, New Hampshire
Telephone: 603-650-1505
Web site: http://www.dartmouth.edu/dms

Mary Hitchcock Memorial Hospital, Norris Cotton Cancer Center, White River Junction Veterans Administration Hospital, Brattleboro Retreat, Family Medical Institute of Augusta, Hartford Hospital, Tuba City Indian Health Service Hospital, primary-care sites in Maine, New Hampshire, and Vermont

New Jersey

University of Medicine and Dentistry of New Jersey–New Jersey Medical School
Newark, New Jersey
Telephone: 973-972-4631
E-mail: njmsadmiss@umdnj.edu
Web site: http://www.umdnj.edu/njmsWeb

University Hospital, East Orange VA Hospital, Hackensack University Medical Center, Morristown Memorial Hospital, Children's Hospital of New Jersey, Kessler Institute, Bergen Pines Hospital

University of Medicine and Dentistry of New Jersey–Robert Wood Johnson Medical School
Piscataway, New Jersey
Telephone: 732-235-4576
Web site: http://www2.umdnj.edu/rwjms.html

Robert Wood Johnson University Hospital, Cooper Hospital/University Medical Center, affiliated community hospitals in central New Jersey

New Mexico

University of New Mexico School of Medicine
Albuquerque, New Mexico
Telephone: 505-272-4766
Web site: http://hsc.unm.edu/som/admiss

University Hospital, Regional Federal Medical Center, UNM Mental Health Center, UNM Children's Psychiatric Hospital, Center for Non-Invasive Diagnosis, international cancer center, family practice center

New York

Albany Medical College
Albany, New York
Telephone: 518-262-5521

Web site: http://www.amc.edu

Albany Medical Center Hospital, Albany Veterans Administration Medical Center, Capital District Psychiatric Center, affiliated area hospitals

Albert Einstein College of Medicine of Yeshiva University

Bronx, New York

Telephone: 718-430-2106

E-mail: admissions@aecom.yu.edu

Web site: http://www.aecom.yu.edu

Jacobi Medical Center, Beth Israel Medical Center, Montefiore Medical Center, Bronx Lebanon Hospital Center, Long Island Jewish Medical Center, affiliated hospices and neighborhood health centers in the Bronx, Queens, and Manhattan

Columbia University College of Physicians and Surgeons

New York, New York

Telephone: 212-305-3595

Web site: http://www.columbia.edu/dept/ps

Columbia-Presbyterian Medical Center, Roosevelt–St. Luke's Hospital Center, Harlem Hospital Center, Bassett Hospital, Overlook Hospital

Mount Sinai School of Medicine of the City University of New York

New York, New York

Telephone: 212-241-6696

Web site: http://www.mssm.edu

Mount Sinai Hospital, affiliated municipal hospitals, VA Medical Center, private community hospitals, private practitioners

New York Medical College

Valhalla, New York

Telephone: 914-594-4507

Web site: http://www.nymc.edu

More than twenty affiliated hospitals in the New York City metropolitan area

New York University School of Medicine

New York, New York

Telephone: 212-263-5290

Web site: http://www.med.nyu.edu

State University of New York at Stony Brook School of Medicine Health Sciences Center

Stony Brook, New York

Telephone: 516-444-2113

E-mail: admissions@dean.som.sunysb.edu

Web site: http://www.hsc.sunysb.edu/som

University Hospital, affiliated clinical facilities

State University of New York Health Science Center at Brooklyn College of Medicine

Brooklyn, New York

Telephone: 718-270-2446

E-mail: admissions@netmail.hscbklyn.edu

Web site: http://www.hscbklyn.edu

University Hospital, several major affiliated community hospitals

State University of New York Health Science Center at Syracuse College of Medicine

Syracuse, New York

Telephone: 315-464-4570

University of Buffalo School of Medicine and Biomedical Sciences

Buffalo, New York

Telephone: 716-829-3466

E-mail: jrosso@acsu.buffalo.edu

Web site: http://wings.buffalo.edu/smbs

Nine affiliated area hospitals

University of Rochester School of Medicine and Dentistry

Rochester, New York

Telephone: 716-275-4539

E-mail: mdadmish@urmc.rochester.edu

Web site: http://www.urmc.rochester.edu/smd

Strong Memorial Hospital, Ambulatory Care Center, five affiliated community hospitals

Weill Medical College of Cornell University

New York, New York

Telephone: 212-746-1067

Web site: http://www.med.cornell.edu

New York Presbyterian Hospital, Memorial Sloan–Kettering Cancer Center, Hospital for Special Surgery, New York Hospital Medical Center of Queens, New York Community Hospital of Brooklyn, St. Barnabas Hospital, Lincoln Medical and Mental Health Center, Wykoff Heights Medical Center, Burke Rehabilitation Center, United Hospital Medical Center, Cayuga Medical Center

North Carolina

Duke University School of Medicine

Durham, North Carolina

Telephone: 919-684-2985

Web site: http://www.mc.duke.edu/depts/som

Duke Hospital, Durham Veterans Administration Hospital

East Carolina University School of Medicine

Greenville, North Carolina

Telephone: 252-816-2202

Web site: http://www.med.ecu.edu/htdocs/admiss/som.htm

Pitt County Memorial Hospital, Leo W. Jenkins Cancer Center, Child Development Evaluation Clinic, Mental Health Center, Alcoholic Rehabilitation Center, Rehabilitation Center, Area Health Education Center, Intensive/Intermediate Care Neonatal Unit

University of North Carolina at Chapel Hill School of Medicine

Chapel Hill, North Carolina

Telephone: 919-962-8331

E-mail: admissions@med.unc.edu

Web site: http://www.med.unc.edu

University Hospitals, Cancer Research Center, Area Health Education Centers throughout the state

Wake Forest University School of Medicine

Winston-Salem, North Carolina

Telephone: 336-716-4264

E-mail: medadmit@wfubmc.edu

Web site: http://www.wfubmc.edu

North Carolina Baptist Hospitals, Inc.; Forsyth Memorial Hospital; Reynolds Health Center; Northwest Area Health Education Center

North Dakota

University of North Dakota School of Medicine and Health Sciences

Grand Forks, North Dakota

Telephone: 701-777-4221

E-mail: judy.heit@mail.med.und.nodak.edu

Web site: http://www.med.und.nodak.edu

Affiliated community physicians, clinics, and hospitals

Ohio

Case Western Reserve University School of Medicine

Cleveland, Ohio

Telephone: 216-368-3450

Web site: http://mediswww.cwru.edu

University Hospitals of Cleveland, MetroHealth Medical Center, St. Luke's Hospital, Veterans Affairs Cleveland Medical Center, Mt. Sinai Medical Center, Henry Ford Health System

Medical College of Ohio

Toledo, Ohio

Telephone: 419-383-4229

Web site: http://wwww.mco.edu

Area Health Education Center, Henry Ford Health System

Northeastern Ohio Universities College of Medicine

Rootstown, Ohio

Telephone: 330-325-6270 or 800-686-2511 (toll-free)

E-mail: admission@neoucom.edu

Web site: http://www.neoucom.edu

Sixteen affiliated community hospitals in the greater Akron, Youngstown, and Canton areas

Ohio State University College of Medicine and Public Health

Columbus, Ohio

Telephone: 614-292-7137

E-mail: admiss-med@osu.edu

Web site: http://www.med.ohio-state.edu

University Hospitals, Arthur James Cancer Hospital and Research Institute, Cleveland Clinic Foundation, outpatient facilities network, affiliated small-town and rural hospitals and clinics

University of Cincinnati College of Medicine

Cincinnati, Ohio

Telephone: 513-558-7314

Web site: http://www.med.uc.edu

College of Medicine, Children's Hospital Medical Center

Wright State University School of Medicine

Dayton, Ohio

Telephone: 937-775-2934

E-mail: som_saa@desire.wright.edu

Web site: http://www.med.wright.edu

Seven affiliated major teaching hospitals

Oklahoma

University of Oklahoma College of Medicine
Oklahoma City, Oklahoma
Telephone: 405-271-2331
E-mail: dotty-shaw@ouhsc.edu
Web site: http://www.ouhsc.edu

Oklahoma Health Center, several affiliated hospitals in the Tulsa area, rural preceptorships

Oregon

Oregon Health Sciences University School of Medicine
Portland, Oregon
Telephone: 503-494-2998
Web site: http://www.ohsu.edu/som-Dean/admit.html

University Hospitals, Outpatient Clinic, Crippled Children's Division, Child Development and Rehabilitation Center, Veterans Administration Hospital

Pennsylvania

Jefferson Medical College of Thomas Jefferson University
Philadelphia, Pennsylvania
Telephone: 215-955-6983
E-mail: jmc.admissions@mail.tju.edu
Web site: http://www.tju.edu

University Hospital, fifteen affiliated federal and community hospitals

MCP Hahnemann University School of Medicine
Philadelphia, Pennsylvania
Telephone: 215-991-8202
E-mail: admis@mcphu.edu

AHERF system hospitals, affiliated hospitals and clinics

Pennsylvania State University College of Medicine

Hershey, Pennsylvania

Telephone: 717-531-8755

E-mail: hmcsaff@psu.edu

Web site: http://www.collmed.psu.edu

Milton S. Hershey Medical Center, Children's Hospital, Rehabilitation Hospital, Center for Emergency Medical Services, and other Penn State Geisinger Health System facilities; Penn State Center for Sports Medicine

Temple University School of Medicine

Philadelphia, Pennsylvania

Telephone: 215-707-3656

Web site: http://www.temple.edu/medschool

Temple Hospital, University Hospital, Temple University Children's Medical Center, Albert Einstein Medical Center, twenty-three affiliated Pennsylvania hospitals

University of Pennsylvania School of Medicine

Philadelphia, Pennsylvania

Telephone: 215-898-8001

Web site: http://www.med.upenn.edu/admiss

Hospital of the University of Pennsylvania, Children's Hospital of Philadelphia, Veterans Administration of Philadelphia Hospitals, Presbyterian Medical Center of Philadelphia, Pennsylvania Hospital, Phoenixville Hospital

University of Pittsburgh School of Medicine

Pittsburgh, Pennsylvania

Telephone: 412-648-9891

E-mail: admissions@fsl.dean-med.pitt.edu

Web site: http://www.dean_med.pitt.edu

UPMC Presbyterian and UPMC Shadyside Hospitals, Western Psychiatric Institute and Clinic, Eye & Ear, Magee-Women's Hospital, UPMC Rehabilitation Hospital, Children's Hospital of Pittsburgh, Veterans Affairs Medical Centers, nine regional community hospitals

Puerto Rico

Ponce School of Medicine

Ponce, Puerto Rico
Telephone: 787-840-2511

Damas Hospital, La Playa Diagnostic Center, Ponce District Hospital, Dr. Pila Hospital, St. Luke's Hospital, Concepcion Hospital, Yauco Regional Hospital

Universidad Central del Caribe School of Medicine

Bayam-n, Puerto Rico
Telephone: 787-740-1611 Ext. 210
Web site: http://www.uccaribe.edu

Dr. Ram-n Ru'z Arnau University Hospital

University of Puerto Rico School of Medicine

San Juan, Puerto Rico
Telephone: 787-758-2525 Ext. 5213
E-mail: raponte@rcmaxp.upr.clu.edu

Affiliated hospitals of the Puerto Rico Medical Center and the Hospital Consortium

Rhode Island

Brown University School of Medicine

Providence, Rhode Island
Telephone: 401-863-2149
E-mail: MedSchool_Admissions@brown.edu
Web site: http://www.brown.edu

Bradley Hospital, Butler Hospital, Memorial Hospital, Miriam Hospital, Rhode Island Hospital, Women and Infants Hospital, Veterans Administration Hospital, Affinity Group mentoring program

South Carolina

Medical University of South Carolina College of Medicine

Charleston, South Carolina

Telephone: 803-792-3283

E-mail: taylorwl@musc.edu

Web site: http://www2.musc.edu

Medical University Hospital, Children's Hospital, Storm Eye Institute, Psychiatric Institute, Holdings Cancer Center, Veterans Administration Hospital, Charleston Memorial Hospital, consortium and community hospitals in Greenville, Spartanburg, Columbia, and Florence

University of South Carolina School of Medicine

Columbia, South Carolina

Telephone: 803-733-3325

Web site: http://www.med.sc.edu

Palmetto Richland Memorial Hospital, William S. Hall Psychiatric Institute, Dorn Veterans Affairs Medical Center, Moncrief Army Hospital, Greenville Memorial Hospital, Area Health Education Consortium, affiliated community hospitals

South Dakota

University of South Dakota School of Medicine

Vermillion, South Dakota

Telephone: 605-677-5233

Web site: http://www.usd.edu/med/som

Yankton, Sioux Falls, and Rapid City clinical training centers; Cardiovascular Research Institute

Tennessee

East Tennessee State University James H. Quillen College of Medicine

Johnson City, Tennessee

Telephone: 423-439-6221

E-mail: sacom@etsu.edu

Web site: http://qcom.etsu.edu

Affiliated hospitals and clinics throughout Tennessee, accelerated residency training programs in family medicine and internal medicine

Meharry Medical College School of Medicine

Nashville, Tennessee
Telephone: 615-327-6228
Web site: http://www.mmc.edu

Metropolitan Nashville General Hospital, York Veterans Administration Medical Center, Blanchfield Community Hospital, Elam Community Medical Center, Murfreesboro Veterans Administration Hospital, affiliated hospitals and clinics

University of Tennessee, Memphis College of Medicine

Memphis, Tennessee
Telephone: 901-448-5559
Web site: http://www.utmem.edu/medicine

University of Tennessee William F. Bowld Hospital, St. Jude Children's Hospital, LeBonheur Children's Hospital, Veterans Administration Hospital, Baptist Memorial Hospital, Regional Medical Center, LePasses Rehabilitation Center, Campbell Clinic, affiliated hospitals and clinics

Vanderbilt University School of Medicine

Nashville, Tennessee
Telephone: 615-322-2145
E-mail: medsch.admis@mcmail.vanderbilt.edu
Web site: http://www.mc.vanderbilt.edu/medschool

University Medical Center, affiliated hospitals

Texas

Baylor College of Medicine

Houston, Texas
Telephone: 713-798-4842
E-mail: melodym@bcm.tmc.edu
Web site: http://www.bcm.tmc.edu/bcm-admissions.html

Texas Medical Center, six affiliated teaching hospitals

Texas A&M University System Health Science Center College of Medicine

College Station, Texas
Telephone: 409-845-7743
E-mail: med-stu-aff@tamu.edu
Web site: http://hsc.tamu.edu

Central Texas Medical Centers, Olin E. Teague Veterans Center, Scott and White Clinic and Hospital, Darnall Army Community Hospital, Driscoll Children's Hospital

Texas Tech University Health Sciences Center School of Medicine

Lubbock, Texas
Telephone: 806-743-2297
Web site: http://www.ttuhsc.edu

Primary teaching hospitals in Lubbock, Amarillo, and El Paso; affiliated community hospitals

University of Texas at San Antonio Medical School

San Antonio, Texas
Telephone: 210-567-2665
E-mail: jonesd@uthscsa.edu
Web site: http://wwwuthscsa.edu

University Hospital, University Health Center, Audie Murphy Veterans Hospital, Wilford Hall USAF Hospital, Brooke Army Hospital, Aerospace Medical Division of USAF, Baptist Memorial Hospital System, Santa Rosa Medical Center

University of Texas–Houston Health Science Center

Houston, Texas
Telephone: 713-500-5116
Web site: http://www.med.uth.tmc.edu

Hermann Hospital, M. D. Anderson Cancer Center, St. Joseph Hospital, San Jose Clinic, Southwest Memorial Hospital, Lyndon Baines Johnson Hospital

University of Texas Medical Branch at Galveston

Galveston, Texas

Telephone: 409-772-3517

E-mail: pwylie@utmb.edu

Web site: http://www.utmb.edu

Eight affiliated hospitals, seventy-five hospital clinics, ninety-three outpatient clinics

University of Texas Southwestern Medical Center at Dallas

Dallas, Texas

Telephone: 214-648-5617

Web site: http://www.swmed.edu

Parkland Memorial Hospital, James Aston Ambulatory Care Center, Zale Lipshy University Hospital, Children's Medical Center, Dallas Veterans Affairs Medical Center, Southwestern Institute of Forensic Sciences, Baylor University Medical Center, Presbyterian Hospital of Dallas, Methodist Hospitals of Dallas, St. Paul Medical Center, Texas Scottish Rite Hospital for Children, John Peter Smith Hospital

Utah

University of Utah School of Medicine

Salt Lake City, Utah

Telephone: 801-581-7498

E-mail: deans.admissions@hs.utah.edu

Web site: http://medstat.med.utah.edu/som

University Hospitals and Clinics, Howard Hughes Medical Institute, Utah Genome Center, Utah Cancer Center, Huntsman Cancer Institute, Moran Eye Center, affiliated centers for special studies

Vermont

University of Vermont College of Medicine

Burlington, Vermont

Telephone: 802-656-2154

Web site: http://www.med.uvm.edu

Fletcher Allen Health Care Medical Center Hospital of Vermont Campus

Virginia

Eastern Virginia Medical School of the Medical College of Hampton Roads
Norfolk, Virginia
Telephone: 757-446-5812
gopher site: gopher://picard.evms.edu/1

More than thirty-three affiliated community-based health-care facilities

University of Virginia School of Medicine
Charlottesville, Virginia
Telephone: 804-924-5571
Web site: http://www.med.virginia.edu/home.html

University Hospital

Virginia Commonwealth University School of Medicine
Richmond, Virginia
Telephone: 804-828-9629
Web site: http://www.vcu.edu

MCV Clinical Research Center

Washington

University of Washington School of Medicine
Seattle, Washington
Telephone: 206-543-7212
E-mail: askuwsom@u.washington.edu
Web site: http://www.washington.edu/medical/som

West Virginia

Marshall University School of Medicine
Huntington, West Virginia

Telephone: 304-691-1738 or 800-544-8514 (toll-free)

*Veterans Affairs Medical Center, Ambulatory Care Center, affiliated
community hospitals, rural clinics, and private physicians*

West Virginia University School of Medicine
Morgantown, West Virginia
Telephone: 304-293-3521
Web site: http://www.hsc.wvu.edu/som

*Ruby Memorial Hospital, Chestnut Ridge Psychiatric Hospital, Health
South Mountainview Regional Rehabilitation Hospital, Cancer Center,
Charleston Division of the Health Sciences Center*

Wisconsin

Medical College of Wisconsin
Milwaukee, Wisconsin
Telephone: 414-456-8246
Web site: http://www.mcw.edu/medschool

*Froedtert Memorial Lutheran Hospital, Clement J. Zablocki Veterans
Affairs Medical Center, Children's Hospital of Wisconsin, affiliated private
and community hospitals*

University of Wisconsin Medical School
Madison, Wisconsin
Telephone: 608-263-4925
Web site: http://www.biostat.wisc.edu

*University Hospital and Clinics, Wisconsin Clinical Cancer Center, affili-
ated clinical sites throughout the state*

OSTEOPATHIC SCHOOLS

Contact the individual schools for current clinical affiliations.

Arizona

**Arizona College of Osteopathic Medicine of
Midwestern University**
Glendale, Arizona
Telephone: 602-572-3215 or 888-247-9277 (toll-free)

California

Touro University College of Osteopathic Medicine
Mare Island, California
Telephone: 707-562-5100 or 888-887-7336 (toll-free in California)
or 888-880-7336 (toll-free outside of California)
E-mail: haight@adminm.touro.edu

**Western University of Health Sciences/College of Osteopathic
Medicine of the Pacific**
Pomona, California
Telephone: 909-623-6116

Florida

**Nova Southeastern University College of Osteopathic Medi-
cine**
Fort Lauderdale, Florida
Telephone: 954-262-1101 or 800-356-0026 Ext. 1101 (toll-free)

Illinois

**Chicago College of Osteopathic Medicine of
Midwestern University**
Downers Grove, Illinois
Telephone: 630-515-6472 or 800-458-6253 (toll-free)
E-mail: Admiss@midwestern.edu
Web site: http://www.midwestern.edu

Iowa

University of Osteopathic Medicine and Health Sciences
College of Osteopathic Medicine and Surgery
Des Moines, Iowa
Telephone: 515-271-1450 or 800-240-2767 Ext. 1450 (toll-free)
E-mail: doadmit@uomhs.edu

Kentucky

Pikeville College of Osteopathic Medicine
Pikeville, Kentucky
Telephone: 606-432-9617 (admissions); 606-432-9640 (student affairs)
E-mail: spayson@pc.edu
Web page: http://www.pc.edu

Maine

University of New England College of Osteopathic Medicine
Biddeford, Maine
Telephone: 800-477-4UNE (toll-free)

Michigan

Michigan State University College of Osteopathic Medicine
East Lansing, Michigan
Telephone: 517-353-7740

Missouri

Kirksville College of Osteopathic Medicine
Kirksville, Missouri
Telephone: 660-626-2237 or 800-626-5266 (toll-free)
Web site: http://www.kcom.edu

The University of Health Sciences College of Osteopathic Medicine
Kansas City, Missouri
Telephone: 800-234-4UHS (toll-free)

New Jersey

University of Medicine and Dentistry of New Jersey School of Osteopathic Medicine
Stratford, New Jersey
Telephone: 609-566-7050
E-mail: somad@umdnj.edu

New York

New York College of Osteopathic Medicine of New York Institute of Technology
Old Westbury, New York
Telephone: 516-686-3747
Web site: http://www.nyit.edu/nycom

Ohio

Ohio University College of Osteopathic Medicine
Athens, Ohio
Telephone: 740-593-4313
Web site: http://www.oucom.ohiou.edu

Oklahoma

Oklahoma State University College of Osteopathic Medicine
Tulsa, Oklahoma
Telephone: 918-582-1972 or 800-677-1972 (toll-free)

Pennsylvania

The Lake Erie College of Osteopathic Medicine
Erie, Pennsylvania
Telephone: 814-866-6641

Philadelphia College of Osteopathic Medicine

Philadelphia, Pennsylvania

Telephone: 800-999-6998 (toll-free)

Web site: http://www.pcom.edu

Texas

University of North Texas Health Science Center

Texas College of Osteopathic Medicine

Fort Worth, Texas

Telephone: 817-735-2204 or 800-535-TCOM (toll-free)

West Virginia

West Virginia School of Osteopathic Medicine

Lewisburg, West Virginia

Telephone: 304-645-6270 or 800-356-7836 (toll-free)

Web site: http://www.wvsom.edu

AMCAS and AACOMAS Sample Applications

Appendix B

The following are excerpts from the American Medical College Application Service (AMCAS) application and the American Association of Colleges of Osteopathic Medicine Application Service (AACOMAS) application.

Appendix B
AMCAS and AACOMAS
Sample Applications

1. SSN		**AMCAS® APPLICATION** **FOR THE 2000 ENTERING CLASS**		AMCAS USE ONLY	

2A. Last Name		2B. First Name	2C. Middle Name	2D. Suffix

3A. Permanent Address - Street	3B. City (and Province)	3C. St	3D. Zip/Postal Code

3E. County (if in U.S.A.)	3F. Country (if not U.S.A.)	4. Telephone ( )

5. PARENTS OR GUARDIAN

Name	Living?		Occupation	Legal Residence	Education/College (highest level)
	Yes	No			
Father					
Mother					
Guardian					

6A. Ages of your Brothers	6B. Ages of your Sisters	7A. Secondary School—Name	7B. Location	7C. Grad Yr.

8. ALL COLLEGES, GRADUATE AND PROFESSIONAL SCHOOLS ATTENDED (list in chronological order)

Name	Location	Dates of Attendance MM/YY MM/YY	Check if summer only	Check if Jr/Comm College	Major	Degree Granted or Expected (with date)
		to to				
		to to				
		to to				
		to to				
		to to				

9 Post-Secondary Honors/Awards:

10. Extracurricular, Community, and Avocational Activities:

11. Chronological Post-Secondary History, including Volunteer, Part-Time and Full-Time Employment

See AMCAS instructions before completing this form.

PERSONAL COMMENTS (Your comments must not exceed the space provided. Use a font at least 10 points in size.)

Name (Last Name First)

COLLEGE NAME LOCATION	ACADEMIC STATUS	BCPM/A	ACADEMIC YEAR	TERM	COURSE NAME	NUMBER	TYPE	TRANSCRIPT GRADE	SEMESTER HOURS ATTEMPTED	AMCAS GRADE	AMCAS USE

14. MCAT Testing Status

Number of MCATs taken since April 1991

Have you taken, or do you plan to take, the August 1999 MCAT?

YES ☐   NO ☐

15. Medical School
You must answer this Question

Have you ever matriculated at or attended any medical school as a candidate for the M.D. degree?

YES ☐   NO ☐

16. Institutional Action
You must answer this Question

[Refer to AMCAS instructions before answering.] Were you ever the recipient of any action (e.g., dismissal, disqualification, suspension, etc.) by any college or medical school for: (1) unacceptable academic performance or (2) conduct violations? If "YES," explain fully in the "Personal Comments" section (page 2).

YES ☐   NO ☐

Certification Statement

I have read and understand the AMCAS instructions. I certify that the information submitted in this application and associated materials is current, complete, and accurate to the best of my knowledge.

SIGNATURE (BLACK INK ONLY)

DATE

No. E-6 Rev. 3/99   -4-   COPYRIGHT 1999 BY THE ASSOCIATION OF AMERICAN MEDICAL COLLEGES

AMCAS® DESIGNATION FORM FOR THE 2000 ENTERING CLASS

| AMCAS USE ONLY |

1. Social Security Number

2. Last Name

First Name

Middle Name

Suffix

3. Area Code/Telephone Number

4. Preferred Mailing Address

City (and Province)

State

Zip Code/ Postal Code

Country

Internet E-Mail Address (Maximum 60 Characters)

5. Legal Residence (Answer even if you are not a U.S. citizen)
State   County Code   County Name

6. Citizenship
Country Name

Country Code

7. Visa Type

8. Sex: M   F

9. Birth Date: Month   Day   Year

10. Age

11. Number of Dependents

12. Birthplace: State   City

County Code   County Name

Country Code   Country Name (If other than U.S.A.)

13. What is your racial/ethnic self-description?
Refer to instructions for codes. Enter only **one** code.

14. Do you identify yourself as a disadvantaged applicant?
Y or N

15. Have you ever performed military service?
Y or N

16. Advisor Information Service (AIS) Release:
(a) The AAMC may provide information regarding my medical school application to the health professions advisor at my U.S. or Canadian *primary undergraduate college*, provided it meets the criteria set forth in the AMCAS instructions.

(b) You may also designate the college code of another eligible U.S. or Canadian college to receive AIS information in addition to your primary undergraduate college. This selection should be a college at which you completed pre-medical requirements and must be listed on your Official Transcript Inventory.

(a) Y or N

(b) College Code Number

17. EARLY DECISION PROGRAM APPLICANTS ONLY: Complete this section to indicate that you are applying as an Early Decision Applicant. You may only designate this **one** school on side two of this form. Enter the code and name of the Early Decision school below:

SCHOOL CODE

SCHOOL NAME (THIS SCHOOL MUST BE THE **ONLY ONE** DESIGNATED ON SIDE 2)

EARLY DECISION DECLARATION: I agree that I will attend my designated Early Decision school if accepted under the Early Decision Program. I also affirm that I have neither submitted, nor will submit an application to any other U.S. medical school (AMCAS or non-AMCAS) for the current entering class, until I have been notified of rejection under the Early Decision Program or the October 1 notification deadline has passed. I certify that I have read and clearly understand the "Regulations of the Early Decision Program" set forth in the AMCAS instructions.

SIGNATURE:_____ DATE:_____

CREDIT CARD INFORMATION
(Complete only if you wish to pay fees by credit card)

Please note that $55 of the AMCAS service fee is non-refundable. Your signature verifies that you have read, understand, and agree to the conditions regarding payment by credit card that are listed on this form and in the AMCAS instructions.

I wish to use: **Visa** or **MasterCard** (circle one) Card Number:_____ Expiration Date:_____

Cardholder's Name:_____ Cardholder's Signature_____

Amount of charge: $_____   Date:_____   Daytime Phone:_____

Side 1 of 2

No E-18   Rev 3/99

AMCAS ® BIOGRAPHIC CHANGE FORM   **DO NOT SUBMIT WITH APPLICATION**

Complete this form to correct or update biographic information. Refer to the AMCAS instructions for codes.
ONLY the biographic items appearing on this form can be altered. No changes can be made to the
information on page one or two of the AMCAS application under any circumstances. Submit this form to:

AMCAS, attn: Biographic Changes
AAMC Section for Student Services
2501 M Street, NW, LBBY-26
Washington, DC 20037-1300
Fax: (202) 828-1120

Allow three weeks for any change to be reviewed, processed, and forwarded to your designated medical schools. A new Transmittal
Notification will be mailed to you when the change is complete. If your requested change cannot be made, you will receive a written
explanation.

ENTERING YEAR | 2 | 0 | 0 | 0 | **SOCIAL SECURITY NUMBER**

Last Name: _____   **First Name:** _____   **MI:** _____

ONLY COMPLETE ITEMS TO BE CHANGED. PRINT CLEARLY.
Do not exceed space provided or enter hyphens, spaces, or other punctuation.

Last Name

First Name   Middle Name   Suffix

Preferred Mailing Address

City (and Province)   State   ZIP Code/Postal Code

Country Code   Country Name (if other than USA)   Area Code   Phone Number

Internet e-mail address (60 characters max):

Legal Residence
State   County Code   County Name   Citizenship
Code   Country Name   Visa Type

Birthdate
Month/Day/Year   Birthplace
State   City Name   Birthplace
County Code   County Name

Sex   # of Dependents   Military Service   Self-Description   Disadvantaged Status

M or F   Y or N   Y or N

ADVISOR INFORMATION SERVICE (AIS) RELEASE

The AIS will automatically forward information to the U.S. or Canadian college awarding your initial Bachelors degree, provided it meets criteria set
forth in instructions. Please designate another "eligible" U.S. or Canadian college (post-baccalaureate program at which you completed pre-medical
requirements, graduate program) to receive AIS information.

Y or N   College Code   College Name   State

AACOMAS Application for the 2000 Entering Class

See AACOMAS Instruction Booklet before completing this form.

1. SSN | | | | | | | | | | | | 2. Name _____
                                                last   *first*   *middle*   *suffix*

3. Do you have educational materials under another name?   Yes [   ]   No [   ]   If yes, indicate name_____

4. Preferred Mailing Address _____
                                      street   *city*
_____ Telephone (   )
      state   *zip code*   *area code*   *number*

5. Permanent and/or Legal Residence_____
                                            street   *city*
_____ Telephone (   )
     county   *state*   *zip code*   *area code*   *number*

6. Are you a U.S. Citizen?   Yes [   ]   No [   ] If No, what is your residency status?   Temporary [   ]   Permanent [   ]

7. Gender*   Male [   ]   Female [   ]   8. Birth Date* | | | | | | | |

9. How do you describe yourself?* (see p.19 - choose only one)   Number | | Letter (if applicable) | | _____

10. Parent/Guardian

	Name	Living Yes No	Occupation	State of Residence	Education/College or highest level
Father	_____	[ ] [ ]	_____		
Mother	_____	[ ] [ ]	_____		
Guardian	_____	[ ] [ ]	_____		

11. Secondary School_____
                       name   *city*   *state*   *year of graduation*

12. A. All Undergraduate Colleges Attended/Planning to Attend (list in chronological order)

College Code	Institution Name	Campus/Location/State	Dates of Attendance	Check if Summer Only	Major	Degree Granted or expected (with date)
___	_____	_____	___ to ___	[ ]	___	___
___	_____	_____	___ to ___	[ ]	___	___
___	_____	_____	___ to ___	[ ]	___	___
___	_____	_____	___	[ ]	___	___
___	_____	_____	___	[ ]	___	___
___	_____	_____	___	[ ]	___	___

B. All Graduate or Professional Schools Attended/Planning to Attend (list in chronological order)

___	_____	_____	___ to ___	[ ]	___	___
___	_____	_____	___ to ___	[ ]	___	___
___	_____	_____	___ to ___	[ ]	___	___

13. Have you had any U.S. military experience?   Yes [   ]   No [   ]   Was your discharge dishonorable? Yes [   ] No [   ]

14. List employment in chronological order, beginning with your current position:

Title or Description	Dates	Level of Responsibility
_____	_____	_____
_____	_____	_____
_____	_____	_____

                                                                           (continue on back)

*See Instruction Booklet   DO NOT TYPE OUTSIDE THE BORDER

                                              FOR OFFICE USE ONLY | | | | | | | |

-3-

SSN |_|_|_|_|_|_|_|_|_| 2. Name_____
                                              last   first   middle   suffix

	College	Location	Year	Term	Number	Course Name	Type	Academic Status	Subject	Semester Hours	AACOMAS Grade	Actual Grade	AACOMAS Use		
49.															
50.															
51.															
52.															
53.															
54.															
55.															
56.															
57.															
58.															
59.															
60.															
61.															
62.															
63.															
64.															
65.															
66.															
67.															
68.															
69.															
70.															
71.															
72.															
73.															
74.															
75.															
76.															
77.															
78.															
79.															
80.															
81.															
82.															
83.															
84.															

*Subject code of "C" is not a valid code

List volunteer positions, internships, etc. (include dates):_____

_____
_____
_____
_____

List honors and/or awards if applicable:_____

_____
_____
_____
_____

Test Scores				
Date	Verbal	Phys Sci	Writing	Biology

How many times have you taken the MCAT test?	☐	If you plan to take or retake the MCAT — enter date.	☐ Mo.	☐ yr.

14. Employment (continued)

Title or Description	Dates	Level of Responsibility

It is imperative you answer # 15-19. If # 16-18 are "yes," # 19 is "F," or # 21 is "31-33" explain in Personal Comments

15. Have you ever matriculated in or attended any medical school as a candidate for the M.D. or D.O. degree? Yes [　] No [　]

16. Were you ever the recipient of <u>any</u> action for unacceptable academic performance (e.g. academic probation, dismissal, suspension, disqualification, etc.) <u>or</u> were you ever the recipient of any action for conduct violations (e.g. probation, suspension, dismissal, etc.) by any college or school? See instruction Booklet.. Yes [　] No [　]

　　If yes, were you ever denied readmission?　　Yes [　]　　No [　]

17. Have you ever been convicted of a misdemeanor or felony (exclude parking violation)? .... Yes [　] No [　]
If you have a pending misdemeanor or felony, which results in a conviction, it is your responsibility to immediately inform a college of osteopathic medicine if you matriculate to that college.

18. Is a family member a D.O. or M.D.? (If yes, list up to three codes from the Instruction Booklet) ..... Yes [　][　][　] No [　]

19. How did you first learn about osteopathic medicine? (choose only one, see Instruction Booklet) ....[　]

20. Have you ever met with an osteopathic college or AACOM representative? (choose only one, see Instruction Booklet)..............[　]

21. Do you consider yourself disadvantaged? (see Instruction Booklet for definition and codes) ....[　]

22. Which choice best describes your prior career/experience? (see Instruction Booklet for definition and codes) ....[　]

PERSONAL COMMENTS/PERSONAL STATEMENT (see AACOMAS Instruction Booklet before completing)

I authorize AACOMAS to release the following information to pre-professional health advisors to assist those advisors in counseling students: my name; the osteopathic medical school at which I matriculate; my state or country of legal residence, as stated in my application materials; my undergraduate institution; and degree date from that institution .... Yes [　] No [　]

I have read and understand the instructions and other information in the AACOMAS Instruction Booklet, and consent to release of information provided or otherwise obtained in the course of the application process to the Colleges of Osteopathic Medicine (in the case of AACOMAS Reports, also with the AAMC). I certify that the information submitted in these application materials is complete and correct to the best of my knowledge. I agree that this information may be used by AACOM, its member institutions, and related health organizations for research and development purposes aimed at improving osteopathic medical education and admissions programs.

Date _____　　Signature _____

2000 ENTERING CLASS - AACOMAS COLLEGE DESIGNATION FORM - Side 1

NOTE: Please refer to the instruction sheet. Print neatly within boxes or fill in the bubble completely using black ink.

Social Security Number

Last Name

First Name

Middle Name

Suffix

Street Address - Mailing

City - Mailing

State - Mailing

Zip - Mailing

Is your mailing address the same as your legal address?
O YES   O NO
Please mark your answer **within** the bubble

Self-description code

Number   Letter
(if applicable)

Street Address - Legal Residence

City - Legal Residence

State - Legal Residence

Zip - Legal Residence

@

E-Mail Address. Please put periods in their own box

State of
Legal Residence

Code for **County**
of Legal Residence

Citizenship Code
(U.S. is 216)

State Where Born

Code for
County of Birth

Code for
Country of Birth

College Code	Major	Major	Degree	MO	YR
				Degree Date	

College Code	Major	Major	Degree	MO	YR
				Degree Date	

College Code	Major	Major	Degree	MO	YR
				Degree Date	

College Code	Major	Major	Degree	MO	YR
				Degree Date	

College Code	Major	Major	Degree	MO	YR
				Degree Date	

College Code	Major	Major	Degree	MO	YR
				Degree Date	

College Code	Major	Major	Degree	MO	YR
				Degree Date	

College Code	Major	Major	Degree	MO	YR
				Degree Date	

College Code	Major	Major	Degree	MO	YR
				Degree Date	

College Code	Major	Major	Degree	MO	YR
				Degree Date	

E

15744

Sample Application Essays

ESSAY 1

I am a 26-year-old woman who has spent much of the past nine years engaged in such unusual activities as jumping out of airplanes, briefing Chuck Yeager (on more effective flying, of all things!), running through trenches, being a test parachutist, taking apart and then reassembling (blindfolded) a vintage M-1 rifle, earning a pilot's license, and learning how to survive behind enemy lines (including resisting interrogations and escaping captivity). All of this has occurred within the context of my time in the military, which began when I enrolled as a cadet at the Air Force Academy in Colorado Springs, Colorado.

Even then I was drawn to science, selecting biology as my major. My freshman year, when I was a lowly "doolie" (a slang derivative of the Latin word meaning "slave"), my grades suffered as I went through the traditional trials of being a first-year military student. It is a psychologically cruel and dehumanizing process (and an existence almost incomprehensible to anyone on the outside) which one must somehow endure while also meeting a full load of academic requirements. The isolation and rigidity of military life made the remaining three years a challenge as well. I frequently tell people that attending the Air Force Academy provided me the best experience of my life (in giving me discipline and showing me the stuff of which I was made) and also the worst.

At the time I graduated, I had a five-year obligation to the Air Force. Despite my continuing interest in becoming a physician, I decided first to fulfill this obligation so I would later be completely free to chart my own course. I chose to become a physiologist with the Air Force because this enabled me to combine my interest in aircraft and aerospace with my fascination with medicine. For two years I ran the hypobaricor altitude chamber, teaching flyers how to use their bodies to be better test pilots. During this same period I earned a master's in systems management, which I felt would help me do my job more effectively. For the past two years, I have been a human factors engineer, testing and making recommendations on equipment so its design produces optimal human performance. At night I teach scuba diving and, in line with my view that a doctor's proper role is at least partly educational, am earning a teaching credential.

With my military service scheduled to come to an end soon, it is finally possible for me to realize my long-held dream of applying to medical school. While my experience since graduating from the Air Force Academy has been highly instructive, it has reinforced my conviction that I am best suited to a career in which personal and human considerations are given highest priority. The interpersonal aspect of the profession holds great appeal for me, as does the fact that the doctor's actions have a direct and significant impact on another human's life. The constant intellectual challenge, the decision-making demands, the fast pace, and the fact that doctors can see the outcome of their work are other elements which attract me.

I know that I have a highly unconventional history for someone aspiring to become a doctor, but I also know that I have what it takes to succeed. My background has taught me many lessons, including, perhaps ironically, the value of human life and the importance of human dignity.

ESSAY 2

Sometimes I like to tell people that my father knew I wanted to be a doctor long before I did, but the truth is that the idea of becoming a physician has probably been gestating within me in some form or other since an early age. There are childhood scenes involving my father, who is a pediatrician, that are indelibly etched in my memory. When I was eight, for example, a young woman came to our door with her first baby, who she thought was dying. My father examined the infant, reassured the mother that there was no serious problem, and sent both away in a state of relief. I also remember, a few years later, being in a restaurant where a woman was choking. "Is there a doctor in the house?" someone asked. My father came forward and took the appropriate steps to help the woman in distress. In both of these instances, as well as many others through the years, I was impressed with my father's capacity to apply his knowledge and skill in a way that made such an important difference in others' lives. He seemed powerful, not in the same way as men who run companies or nations, but as someone who could provide comfort, quiet fears, touch a life, resolve a crisis.

I idolize my father and admire his commitment and contributions, but this alone would not be enough to make me want to become a doctor myself. As I matured, I had a chance to weigh other options and to take a long, hard look at myself, my capabilities, and interests. What I discovered, in time, was that medicine was indeed the most appropriate career path for me, the one best suited to me intellectually, emotionally, and otherwise. For the last four years I have worked one day a week in my father's office, which has given me the chance to interact with patients (and their mothers), observe my father at work, and better understand the dynamics of his practice. Just as when I managed a sandwich shop in high school and had to learn to deal with the public, within his office I have also had to be diplomatic. I have had to relate to many different types of people, often at very vulnerable moments in their lives, and do so with sensitivity and compassion.

Two summers ago I worked as an orderly in the operating room at a hospital in the Los Angeles area. I was there a minimum of 40 scheduled hours a week, and was on call each weekend. My experience at the hospital also gave me exposure to the constant pressure of emergency situations, in which there is little tolerance for error or indecision. And I was pleased to discover that I was more fascinated than repelled by the actual sight of surgery. I saw the delivery of babies, the treatment of gunshot wounds, hysterectomies, and a host of other procedures. I was spellbound by what I saw, and I returned to my premed studies with even greater enthusiasm and focus.

I have always been a very inquisitive person, as well as one who delights in taking things apart and putting them back together. I cannot help but wonder if these aspects of my personality do not somehow relate to my interest in medicine. I know for certain that I am highly attracted to the intellectual component of the profession and the fact that constant learning is such an integral part of being an effective physician. I also happen to find great pleasure in the company of other people, and I like the one-on-one facet of the physician's work.

As directed as I am in terms of my career, my life would be empty without my family, my close friends (most of whom I have known since high school), my girlfriend, and the sports in which I involve myself with great regularity. These are vital elements of my existence and help me to maintain the balance I need.

My family is very warm and loving, and I think they have nurtured in me these same qualities. Each has taken very independent and ambitious paths. My mother has recently become a lawyer; one sister is becoming a psychologist and the other sister a lawyer. My feeling about the future is that if, for any reason, I did not become a doctor, I would be wasting something—namely, my compassion, commitment, energy, and potential to contribute.

ESSAY 3

In 1979, in the Soviet city of Odessa on the Black Sea, a young man confronted a problem that would forever alter the course of his existence. This 17-year-old Jewish man, who wanted most to become a doctor, was denied the possibility of admission to medical school because of his religion. It could have been an end to a dream.

I was that man. My determination to become a physician, and my parents' support of that ambition, turned our lives upside down. We applied for a visa to leave Russia; while we waited, my parents and older brother were not allowed to work, and all of us were followed by the KGB. When we finally arrived in America in 1980, we had to make our way to Seattle without funds, friends, or command of English. My father, who is an engineer, was reduced to working as a plumber, while I began each day at 5 a.m. unloading trucks. Life was a struggle, but we were all sustained by a dream: my goal of studying to become a doctor.

Within a year of my arrival here, after attending night school to learn the language, I was able to obtain a job as an X-ray orderly at a local hospital. In this position, and later as an admitting aide, I was able over a period of three years to learn much more about American medicine. I had extensive contact with patients, doctors, nurses, and administrators and found I was able to relate well to each group. I saw suffering, healing, death, and all of the other constants that make up any hospital environment. I had an opportunity to observe surgeries, from mastectomies to hysterectomies and bypasses, and to see firsthand the importance of positive doctor-patient interactions. I was fascinated by everything I saw and became more convinced than ever that I could one day make my finest contribution as a physician.

When I first entered college, I had enormous problems with English, especially scientific terminology, and my GPA was an unremarkable 2.84. However, as I mastered the language, my grades steadily improved; in fact, in the last three quarters I've earned a 3.8 GPA.

Beginning in 1984, I worked as a volunteer in the autopsy room at my university's pathology department, amassing more than 500 hours' experience. Just as the hospital provided me with a chance to observe diagnosis and treatment, the autopsy room gave me a chance to find out what goes wrong, what causes death. In that room it was possible for me to see death, smell it, touch it. I prepared organs for examination by medical students as well as assisted in autopsies and cleaning up. I was even awarded a highly sought-after scholarship in recognition of my work.

I first became interested in medicine in high school, when I sat in on my brother's medical school lectures and later accompanied him on hospital rounds. My commitment to becoming a doctor, and my excitement over the prospect of being able to serve others in this capacity, is what has driven me and kept me going in the face of so many obstacles since my departure from Russia. Now, with my goal in sight and so many recent experiences reaffirming my passion for medicine, I know that all of the dedication and sacrifice have been worthwhile. I am eager to begin my medical studies, eager to meet the challenges I know they will present.

ESSAY 4

Martial arts and medicine. They seem worlds apart, but they both have played significant roles in my life and for reasons that are surprisingly similar. They both offer challenge, require great discipline, and necessitate a goal-oriented approach.

I first became involved with the martial arts when I was only 13 years old. At that time I began studying karate in my hometown in northern California. Even then I was a goal-oriented individual who was attracted to the step-by-step progression involved in studying karate. Within a year I had earned a brown belt (the next-to-highest ranking) and was actually serving as an instructor at the karate academy where I had learned the sport. Dedication, discipline, and physical and mental prowess were behind my success, which included being the youngest person in the area to attain the brown belt.

In college I became involved in Tae Kwon Do, which is the Korean counterpart of karate. This sport, too, requires patience, determination, and a clear mind in addition to physical strength, endurance, and agility. Within a year I had become president of my university's 80-member Tae Kwon Do club, which ranks among the top sports clubs on campus. In assuming this position I began to have the opportunity to test myself as a leader as well as an athlete.

One of the reasons I became interested in medicine is that it, too, requires a meticulous, goal-oriented approach that is very demanding. Of course, it also happens that the substance of the profession holds strong appeal for me, both in terms of the science and the potential for serving others who are in need.

Most of my exposure to the profession has occurred within the areas of surgery and emergency medicine. After first serving as an emergency medicine volunteer technician at a northern California hospital (where I had a moving experience with a young girl's death), I acquired the EMT-1A/CPR certifications and then worked as an Emergency Medical Technician-1A during a subsequent summer. This job was a fascinating, educational, and high-pressure experience that exposed me to the realities of medicine as practiced in crisis situations.

My extensive involvement with cardiothoracic surgery research over the last three years, first as a volunteer technician and currently as a staff research technician, has further fueled my desire to become a physician. I have had to rely upon my own ingenuity and problem-solving skills as well as what I have learned in the classroom, and this has been exciting. One of the more unusual aspects of my work has involved me directly in the procedure of heterotopic heart transplantation in rats. This precise and technically demanding procedure encompasses microsurgery and usually is conducted only by residents. In fact, I am the only undergraduate student doing this procedure, which has shown me the extent of both my manual dexterity and capacity for learning sophisticated techniques.

I have been fortunate enough to have had the opportunity to participate and contribute in almost every way during experiments, from administering anesthesia and performing extensive surgical preparations to analyzing the data obtained and operating monitoring and recording equipment, ventilators, and the heart-lung machine.

I am a somewhat shy individual, but I have found that within the medical environment that shyness evaporates. The opportunity to help others one-on-one is so rewarding and comfortable for me that I feel very much at ease, regardless of with whom I am working.

I think one of the particularly attractive aspects of medicine for me, especially within such specialties as internal medicine and obstetrics/gynecology, is the potential for forming close, lasting, meaningful relationships with a wide array of patients.

For me, medicine emerges as the perfect avenue for indulging my impulses to contribute, to be involved with science, and to establish important links with others at both critical and noncritical moments in their lives.

Useful Web Sites

See Appendix A for medical school Web sites.

GENERAL WEB SITES

American Association of Colleges of Osteopathic Medicine (AACOM)
http://www.aacom.org

The American Medical Association Fellowship and Residency Electronic Interactive Database (AMA–FREIDA)
http://www.ama-assn.org/freida

American Medical Women's Association (AMWA)
http://www.amwa-doc.org

Association of American Medical Colleges (AAMC)
http://www.aamc.org

CSC Credit Service (credit bureau)
http://www.csc.com/industries/credit/consumer.html

Gay and Lesbian Medical Association
http://www.glma.org

MEDLINE (National Library of Medicine database)
http://www.nlm.nih.gov

National Association of Advisors for the Health Professions (NAAHP)
http://www.naahp.org

Ontario Medical School Application Service (OMSAS)
http://www.ouac.on.ca

Trans Union Corporation (credit bureau)
http://www.tuc.com

FINANCIAL AID WEB SITES

AMWA (Medical Education Loan Program, Wilhelm-Frankowski Medical Education Scholarship)
http://www.amwa-doc.org

Free Application for Federal Student Aid (FAFSA)
http://www.fafsa.ed.gov

National Association of Financial Aid Administrators
http://www.finaid.prg

U.S. Department of Education
http://www.ed.gov

Print
Resources
Used in This
Volume

Appendix E

AACOM. 1999. *Osteopathic Medical College Information Booklet: 2000 Entering Class.* Chevy Chase, MD: author.

AAMC. 1994. *Financial Planning and Management Manual for U.S. Medical Students.* Washington, DC: author.

AAMC. 1999. *Medical School Admission Requirements: United States and Canada, 2000–2001.* Washington, DC: author.

Brink, S. 1999. Caring for the neglected: Areas untouched by a physician surplus. *U.S. News Online.* http://www.usnews.com/usnews/edu/beyond/grad/gbmed.htm

Ferdinand, B., ed. 1999. *Peterson's Gold Standard MCAT.* Princeton, NJ: Peterson's.

Johnson, L. M., ed. 1998. *Minority Student Opportunities in United States Medical Schools: 1998.* 14th ed. Washington, DC: AAMC.

Oransky, I., Poulsen, E. J., Sanghavi, D. M., and Varma, J. K., eds. 1999. *The Insider's Guide to Medical Schools: Current Students Tell You What Their Medical School Is Really Like.* Princeton, NJ: Peterson's.

Peterson's. 1998. *U.S. and Canadian Medical Schools: A Comprehensive Guide to all 159 Accredited Medical Schools.* Princeton, NJ: author.

Porter, R. 1998. *The Greatest Benefit to Mankind: A Medical History of Humanity.* New York: W. W. Norton.

Rohack, J. J. The educational work environment of resident physicians. *Report of the Council on Education.* http://www.ama-assn.org/mem-data/special/mdschool/resenviro.htm

Varner, K. S., ed. 1998. *Curriculum Directory.* 27th ed. Washington, DC: AAMC.

Yacoe, D. 1999. Making the connection: Technology and the evolution of health care at the Mayo Foundation. *The Bond Buyer* September 14:10a.